Keeping Company
with Saint Ignatius

Walking the Camino de
Santiago de Compostela

Luke Larson

Foreword by Chris Lowney

PARACLETE PRESS
BREWSTER, MASSACHUSETTS

2014   First Printing

Keeping Company with Saint Ignatius

ISBN 978-1-61261-519-6

Library of Congress Cataloging-in-Publication Data
Larson, Luke J.
        Keeping   company   with   Saint   Ignatius   :   walking
the Camino de Santiago de Compostela / Luke J. Larson.
        pages cm
    ISBN 978-1-61261-519-6 (pb with french flaps)
    1. Christian pilgrims and pilgrimages—Spain—Santiago de Compostela.
    2. Ignatius, of Loyola, Saint, 1491–1556. 3. Spirituality—Catholic Church.
    4. Spiritual life—Catholic Church. I. Title.
    BX2321.S3L37 2014
    263'.0424611—dc23   2014019346

10 9 8 7 6 5 4 3 2 1

Published by Paraclete Press
Brewster, Massachusetts
www.paracletepress.com
Printed in the United States of America

To Evie, my wife and pilgrim companion.
Thank you for keeping company with me
on the Camino,
and through all of life.

With all my love.

CONTENTS

Foreword

"Our life is a journey, and when we stop moving, things go wrong."

Pope Francis said that, though most would not intuitively associate those sentiments with a pope or the Catholic Church. When we stop moving, things go wrong? The Catholic Church of popular imagination seems to be about the opposite: eternal, unchanging truths and finger-wagging at a modern culture that seems to have lost respect for tradition in its endless fascination with what's new and fashionable.

To be sure, the pope has warned that if we are not grounded in the truths of our tradition, we become aimless wanderers.

But grounded does not mean stuck. And there is a difference between aimless wandering and a purposeful journey, a pilgrimage.

In writing *Pope Francis: Why He Leads the Way He Leads*, I came to understand how deeply the imagery of journey, of pilgrimage, has touched the Pope. He was formed as a Jesuit, and pilgrim imagery is deep in the Jesuit tradition. Ignatius of Loyola, the Jesuit founder, undertook a life-changing, five-hundred-mile personal pilgrimage from his home in Loyola to the towns of Montserrat and Manresa, both near Barcelona. (I worked with a small group to construct a modern pilgrim route tracing the path Ignatius followed; modern-day trekkers can google "Ignatian Camino" or visit caminoignaciano.org to learn more about it.)

Though Ignatius would never have used such trendy terminology, his month-long trek was a journey of self-discovery. Decades after that trek, while dictating his *Autobiography*, Ignatius was still referring to himself as "the pilgrim." What's more, he prescribed the same pilgrim medicine for all future Jesuits: during novitiate, each trainee Jesuit is supposed to undertake a pilgrimage. The requirement, as far as I know, is unique to Jesuit training.

Pope Francis presumably made a pilgrimage during his own training, so perhaps it should not surprise us that journey imagery bubbles up constantly in his talks and writing. Read his talks and note how often words like *journey, pilgrimage, periphery, frontier,* or *margin* all arise. He more than once has said that he far prefers a Church that endures "accidents in the street," because it is out there trying something new, to a Church that is locked in upon itself. He aspires to a Church that is "bruised, hurting, and dirty" because it is accompanying people where they really live, out in the real world.

Well, some of this mindset may trace directly to his own Jesuit formation, but the idea of life as pilgrimage or journey is not uniquely Jesuit. The Catholic tradition, and indeed every great spiritual tradition, seems to have the same wisdom. Devout Muslims are called on pilgrimage to Mecca; the Torah calls the Jewish people to journey to Jerusalem for the so-called pilgrim festivals; Buddhists and Hindus also recognize the tradition of spiritual pilgrimage. And, if we squinted just a little bit, we would also see pilgrimage pretty clearly in what we might call the "secular spirituality" of the United States: a visit to a Civil War-era graveyard may be called a tourist visit, but something more profound is happening. We go to honor those who sacrificed their lives, and, along the way, we think about our own lives.

The idea of pilgrimage is so deeply enshrined in human culture, I suspect, because pilgrimage is the great metaphor for life. Life is a journey. We journey from childhood to senescence. We meet new people along the way, get lost at times, discover things we never knew existed, and learn a lot. We hope that we will get to our destination safely, but we also hope that we will grow and learn something along the way.

Still, those romantic notions notwithstanding, we humans typically resist aspects of the journey, because the journey means change, and we don't like change. We all say we do, but the reality, once we start to settle in to our lives, is different. How intimidating to pack up one's life and move to a new city, start a new career, end an unfulfilling relationship and start a new one, break out of the familiar roles that each family member has settled into and, for example, let *her* be the one who makes the plans for a while and let *him* be the one who manages the household finances. The pope told us that when we stop moving—growing, learning, experimenting, exploring—things go wrong. Yet, truth be told, a lot of us stop moving in some ways.

Pilgrimage can be good medicine for that. Luke Larson appropriately invites us all to hit the road. But he wisely points out that "hitting the road" need not mean the 500-mile journey across Spain that he and his wife undertook to the centuries-old pilgrimage site of Santiago de Compostela. If you have the month, the resources, and gumption to do that, by all means go! (I tried it once, and it remains a life highlight.)

But for many, that will remain one of those "bucket list" dreams that remain forever in the bucket. So, as Luke suggests, do what you can, whether that be walks through unfamiliar parts of the neighborhood, laps around the mall, or a trek from one end of Manhattan to the other, as I do with a few hundred other Catholics each year, ending with Mass at the Mother Seton shrine at Manhattan's southern tip.

I can't explain why this experience of purposeful walking changes us and opens us up, but it does. It just does. When I did my own pilgrimage to Santiago de Compostela, every few days I would run across some New-Age type who would earnestly tell me, "Everyone has something to learn on the Camino." I would smile and fairly quickly change the subject. I love history, love to travel, am a devout Catholic, enjoy a challenge, and looked forward to the exercise. That's why I was going. I wasn't looking to learn something.

Then I got sick halfway through and couldn't finish. I learned what I have to relearn every few years: it's not my world. It's God's world. I'm not in charge of it. It does not revolve around my plans. And even though I behave as if I can control everything that impacts my life, I know I can't. The older we get, the more we understand how little we actually do control.

So, despite myself, I learned something on the Camino. And everyone I know who has gone on pilgrimage has told me they learned something about themselves as well. The good news is that we don't have to wrack our brains in a fervid search for personal revelation. Better if we do the opposite, as Luke suggests. Leave ourselves open to see, listen, and learn, and the insights will come along, in God's good time. After all, it's God's world, not ours.

So hit the road! Whether in your own neighborhood, across Spain to Santiago de Compostela, or along the Camino Ignaciano from Loyola to Manresa, it matters not where you go; it matters that you go. And—to cite the cliché that has by now become hackneyed simply because it is true—it is not about the destination; it's about the journey.

But before you get the chance to savor Luke Larson's wonderful journey, let me offer one last piece of advice, drawn once again from Pope Francis. In a meeting with high school children at the Vatican, one boy spoke of the challenges of growing up and remaining faithful despite the doubts and pressures on a young person nowadays. The pope replied sympathetically, noting that everyone falls along the way. The issue is not in falling, the pope said, but in not staying fallen. That is, get up, and keep going. Don't be discouraged. Failure and difficulty and challenge come to everyone along the way. After speaking to the young boy in this vein for a minute or two, the pope closed with this encouraging message, relevant for all of us: "You won't be afraid of the journey? Thank you."

Chris Lowney

First Steps

Would you like to take a walk?

This question, this personal invitation really, connotes a desire, not to fulfill a goal or reach a destination, but simply to keep company with someone. I imagine it was one of the first questions ever posed.

"Hey, Eve, would you like to take a walk around Eden with me?"

I also imagine that it was one of God's first invitations to us. The book of Genesis tells us that God walked in the garden. On the seventh day, God laid down his power tools, slapped the cosmic dust from his coveralls, and set off looking for our first parents among the ferns and fig trees.

Why? Do you suppose he was in the garden to check up on Adam and Eve, to see what kind of mischief they might be up to? That doesn't sound much like a day of rest to me.

It is not a stretch to assume, as most of us do, that God was there simply to walk and talk with Adam and Eve, to enjoy their company. Respecting human freedom right from the beginning, God would have simply extended an invitation.

"Would you like to walk with me, perhaps in the mornings and evenings when it's nice and cool?"

These walks were not about getting from Point A, say, the Tigris River, to Point B, the Euphrates. They were simply about spending time together, keeping each other company.

What a mind-blowing image: God the Almighty, Creator of heaven and earth, the Alpha and Omega, walking leisurely with Eve and Adam for no other reason than he wanted to. It certainly beats the image of God waiting in the wings listening for the crunch of an apple, his one and only cue to enter the scene.

God is not aloof and distant, showing up only when we are naughty or in need of rescuing. No, God created us good—in his very own image in fact—and likes nothing better than to hang out with us. We were created to live in God's presence. God's desire is always for companionship with us.

This is no less true for us today than it was for our earliest ancestors. By *us* I am not referring to humanity in general, or even to some grouping of humanity, such as the church.

I am talking about you and me specifically.

God the Father wants to be with you no less than he wanted to be with Noah, Abraham, and Moses. God the Son wants to be with you no less than he wanted to be with Peter, John, and Mary Magdalene. God the Holy Spirit wants to be with you no less than he wanted to be with Ezekiel, Jeremiah, and Isaiah. Take a moment and let that sink in. God the Father, Son, and Holy Spirit wants to keep company with you today.

The book of Genesis offers the first images of our Creator's desire to keep company with us. Yet there are plenty of others. Among my favorites is the definitive covenantal summation found in Leviticus: "I will walk among you and be your God, and you will be my people" (Lev. 26:12). Another favorite, from Micah, speaks to what is required of us in that relationship: "To

act justly and to love mercy and to walk humbly with your God"
(Mic. 6:8).

Humble comes from the Latin *humus* meaning "earth." Taken
literally, that means we are to walk with God, not with our head
in the clouds, but *on the ground.* Emmanuel is indeed with us, not
as some ethereal presence, but as a Lover taking a leisurely stroll
with his beloved.

In addition to this more literal meaning of *walk*, the Bible also
uses the word as a metaphor for living in communion with God.
For example, in Deuteronomy, "Walk in obedience to all that the
LORD your God has commanded you, so that you may live and
prosper and prolong your days in the land that you will possess"
(Deut. 5:33) In Ephesians, "Follow God's example . . . as dearly
loved children and walk in the way of love, just as Christ loved us
and gave himself up for us as a fragrant offering and sacrifice to
God" (Eph. 5:1–2). And in 3 John, "I have no greater joy than to
hear that my children are walking in the truth" (3 Jn. 1:4).

Would you like to take a walk?

I wasn't expecting God to saunter up and ask me this in the
garden section of Home Depot. Thankfully, God did not. I
understand such theophanies have rather dire consequences. No,
God chose more typical, and less terrifying, ways to invite my wife
and me to take a walk—a pilgrimage, actually—simply for the sake
of keeping company with us.

The idiom *keeping company* has a number of connotations. It
means spending time with someone so that they are not alone,
accompanying or remaining with someone, associating or staying

connected with someone, and being compassionate to someone. It might also mean being passionate, as in the case of a romantic relationship. All of these are applicable to the walk, the pilgrimage, that my wife, Evie (short for Evelyn), and I made together.

Evie and I walked the Camino Francés, or The French Way, one of the most popular and traditional pilgrimage routes of the Camino de Santiago de Compostela in the fall of 2010. What is the Camino de Santiago de Compostela? Let's begin with a bit of translation. The Spanish *Camino* translates variously as *path, road, journey,* or *way,* while *Santiago* combines *San,* Spanish for *saint,* with the Galician *Iago* for *Jacob* or *James.* Thus we get the *Way of Saint James,* one of the most traveled and revered Christian pilgrimages since the beginning of the tenth century. The *Way* leads to the Cathedral of Santiago de Compostela in Galicia in northwestern Spain where, according to tradition, the remains of Saint James are entombed.

Legend has it that, responding to Jesus's commission to take the Good News of the kingdom to the ends of the earth, James traveled to Finisterre—from the Latin *finis terræ,* literally meaning "end of the earth"—and began his evangelizing work on the Iberian Peninsula. After preaching there for a number of years, James returned to Palestine, where he was beheaded by King Herod Agrippa I in AD 44. The body of James then miraculously made its way back to Galicia in an unmanned boat made of stone. The story continues early in the ninth century when a shepherd discovered James's remains in an unmarked cave. He was drawn to the spot by bright stars in the sky. This brings us to the origin of *Compostela.*

It comes from another combination of Spanish words: *campo* and *stella*, *field* and *star* in English, rendering a *Field of Stars*.

During the Middle Ages hundreds of thousands of people began their arduous journeys to Compostela, to this Field of Stars, from wherever their hometown might be in Europe or beyond.

～

Today many, like us, choose to start their Camino pilgrimages from the small, picturesque town of Saint-Jean-Pied-de-Port on the French side of the Pyrenees. Forty-eight days later, on the eve of All Saints Day, we arrived in the cathedral city of Santiago de Compostela. We made this five-hundred-mile pilgrimage entirely on foot, carrying bare essentials in our lightweight backpacks.

Why did we do it? The pilgrimage was a way of keeping company with God. It was God who invited us, through myriad elicited desires and converged opportunities, to take a walk with him in the first place. God alone initiates the encounter with God. Yet, although God the Father did the inviting, it was God the Son who logged most of the miles with us. Jesus, after all, has the well-worn walking sandals.

Keeping company with Jesus also means keeping company with his friends. One of the more preeminent of these is Saint Ignatius of Loyola, the sixteenth-century founder of the Society of Jesus, commonly known as the Jesuits. If you want to learn about walking as a way of keeping company with Jesus, he's the expert.

More than anything else, Saint Ignatius and his followers wanted to be in the company of Jesus. The first Jesuits described themselves using the Spanish word for companions, *compañeros*, bound together into a company, a *Compagnia di Gesù*, which translates into English as *Society of Jesus*. Jesuits are men, priests, and brothers throughout the world, whose singular and unifying desire is to keep company with Jesus.

For eight years I was counted among their number. And, although it has been almost two decades since I left the Jesuits, the inspiration and spirituality of Ignatius remains the matrix for my life and my loves. Like Ignatius, my deepest desire is to companion Jesus, to keep company with Jesus.

While convalescing from a debilitating leg wound in the ancestral home of the noble Loyola family, Ignatius became attentive to the promptings of the Holy Spirit. He listened to his soul's desire to make a pilgrimage to Jerusalem as soon as he was able. A reproduction of that pilgrimage was to be one of the first communal acts of the early companions of Ignatius. It is fitting, then, that in wanting to revitalize my sense of companionship with Saint Ignatius, I would choose to make a pilgrimage as well. And so Evie and I not only invited Ignatius along with us on the Camino but we dedicated our time in Europe to learning more about his life and legacy.

If I were to choose a saint to companion on a forty-eight-day, five-hundred-mile walking pilgrimage based solely on appearance, I probably would not choose one who is most often portrayed as serious, even dour. Joseph A. Tetlow, SJ, sums up this traditional perception of Ignatius: "He came across as a forbidding personality, icily chaste, intellectually certain beyond challenge, preoccupied with obedience and endowed with iron-willed self-control."[1]

More contemporary depictions, both in artwork and print, shatter some of these cast-in-plaster images we have of Ignatius. Iñigo de Loyola (Ignatius's baptismal name) was the life of the party as a young, courtly cavalier. He was also a bit of a firebrand. There were certainly plenty who wanted to companion him, and to journey with him, after his conversion. So many, in fact, that he formed his fellows into a service-oriented company, which eventually led to the founding of the Society of Jesus in 1540.

On the Feast of the Annunciation in 1534, Ignatius and his first companions professed traditional religious vows of poverty, chastity, and obedience, as well as a fourth vow to go wherever they were requested by the pope. They were ordained to the priesthood in 1537.

A reading of Ignatius's autobiography and numerous letters leaves the impression of a man of humility, gentleness, and deep emotion. For instance, he often wept copious tears while praying and celebrating the Eucharist. He had the most ardent love and affection for his ever-increasing band of brothers, as only a saint could. In fact, he is said to have cheered despondent companions by performing spontaneous Basque dances.[2]

Ignatius was no pushover though. He sternly reprimanded any who showed signs of conceit or strayed from the demands of their religious vows, especially obedience. That being said, keenly aware of human frailty, Ignatius exhibited remarkable patience and flexibility as long as he observed one moving toward—or at least having the desire to move toward—the "praise, reverence and service of God our Lord."[3] In the mind of Ignatius, that is the one absolute and invariable end toward which all of our actions are to be directed. He did not stop there. The Saint used the Latin word *magis,* meaning "more," to exhort others to ever greater generosity for the sake of the greater glory to God, *ad majorem Dei gloriam* in Latin.

Ignatius was on the go for much of his life, except for the times when his health or the demands of his role as the first superior general of the Society of Jesus caused him to stay in Rome. He often traveled by foot, even barefoot, as an ascetical practice. A sampling of his destinations includes Azpeitia, Pamplona, Montserrat, Manresa, Barcelona, Venice, the Holy Land, Genoa, Alcalá, Salamanca, Bologna, Paris, and Rome.

Ignatius expected his companions to adopt his pilgrim spirit of "one foot on the road, ready to hasten from one place to another."[4] To this day, Jesuits are to be contemplatives-in-action, possessing the ability to reflect on the move. "The road is our home," affirmed Jerónimo Nadal, one of Ignatius's early companions.[5]

On many of his trips, Ignatius either crossed over or followed the Camino pilgrimage route, so he had occasions to walk, eat, and rest with pilgrims on their way to Santiago de Compostela. Given his desire to engage in spiritual conversations, and the likelihood of finding other pilgrims predisposed to the same, one can imagine the kinds of interactions he might have had.

"Was not your heart burning before the tomb of Saint Martin in Tours?"

"What holy desires were elicited in you before the fragment of the True Cross in the Church of San Pedro de la Rúa in Estella?"

"Did the face of Santa María de los Arcos in the Church of Santa María de la Asunción move you to tears as well?"

This is the man I wanted to keep company with on our pilgrimage. I wanted the companionship of a saint of heaven, one who had led a very human life on earth. And one who shared my fondness for praying on my feet. I like to think that Saint Ignatius, who often referred to himself in the third person as "the Pilgrim," was pleased to be invited to accompany us on our pilgrimage.

It might seem strange to make a pilgrimage with the traditional intention of visiting the remains of Saint James as a way of companioning another saint, Ignatius of Loyola. As patron of the Camino, Saint James offers his help and protection to anyone who undertakes the pilgrimage with sincerity of heart. James, in Latin *Jacobus*, is called "the Greater" to distinguish him from another apostle named James, "the Lessor." James and his brother John were together nicknamed "the Sons of Thunder" by Jesus.

Evie and I were certainly grateful for the apostle's inspiration, guidance, and presence with us. We enjoyed reading and hearing stories about James before and during our trip. Many of the stories recount "minor miracles" attributed to the intercession of the saint. For instance, a lost wallet is returned by another pilgrim who, days later, happens to stop at the same hostel. Or the pain and inflammation of tendonitis suddenly goes away, enabling a pilgrim to continue on to Santiago.

Some would dismiss such occurrences as mere coincidences or accidents. Others might look on them as reassuring indications of James's big-brotherly presence on the Camino. I'm not sure if such instances are truly *miraculous*—suspending the laws of nature— yet I appreciate any hints of the Son of Thunder's benevolent companionship, not just during the *Reconquista* (the Reconquest) of history, but here and now. On a walking journey of over five hundred miles, I was grateful for any support that came my way, whatever its source.

We eagerly searched for statues of Saint James the Pilgrim in the churches and plaza squares. And we were disturbed when we found instead graphic depictions of a sword-wielding Saint James atop a menacing white horse—*Matamoros*, killer of Moors—even as we understood the historical context of the attributions.

The soldier-turned-pilgrim Ignatius of Loyola relished being in the presence of the saints of heaven during his pilgrimage through this life. So I imagine that he did not mind that we were also keeping company with Saint James the Pilgrim as we trekked across his Basque homeland of northern Spain, savoring the people and places so important in his mind and heart, and in my own, as a former Jesuit.

There were practical reasons for choosing this medieval pilgrimage route as well. Over the past two decades the number of pilgrims traveling the Camino has increased exponentially. Over 272,000 people traveled the Camino in 2010. In order to accommodate them, the number of pilgrim hostels (*albergues* or *refugios*) has likewise increased. So we chose the Camino as a well-traveled, relatively safe, signposted pilgrimage route along which we could count on inexpensive lodging, exclusively reserved for pilgrims, at least every nine miles.

Paraphrasing the Chinese philosopher Lao-tzu (604 BC–531 BC), every journey begins with a single step. Our pilgrimage was a journey of over a million steps. The number of footfalls counts as naught, however. What's important is, from the beginning, God has taken the first steps to walk with us. And from the first steps of the Camino de Santiago to the last, Jesus and his friend Ignatius accompanied us every step of the way.

ONE

My Journey to the Camino de Santiago

I am a cradle Catholic. I've never really had a crisis of faith. Oh, I have experienced crises in life, but these have brought me closer to God, not further apart. It would be an untruth and discredit to the Giver of this unmerited gift to claim otherwise.

My mother is a descendant of Catholic Luxembourg immigrants who had settled her hometown in southwestern Minnesota. The roots of her Catholicism are in Bellechester, but it was at the College of Saint Benedict where my mother's faith was imbued with Benedictine tradition. Next to the large crucifix in our family home hung a painting of Saint Benedict with the words "*ora et labora*" beneath, indicating the activities (prayer and work) to which Benedictine monks dedicate their lives. It was from this faith perspective that my siblings and I were nurtured and educated.

Having been raised a nonpracticing Lutheran on the front range of the Rockies in Montana, my father did not overtly participate in our religious formation. And yet he helped ensure that our First Communions and Confirmations were special occasions. My father entered the Catholic Church when I was a sophomore in high school.

My brothers, sister, and I were taught as children to bow our heads while passing by Catholic churches. We were instructed to do this in acknowledgement of the truth, beyond any doubt, that Jesus Christ is in every Catholic church. More specifically, Jesus is in the tabernacle. As a young child I was curious how Jesus fit inside the ornate golden vessel centered above the back altar but simply accepted it as a matter of faith. I continue the reverential practice of bowing my head while passing by Catholic churches. That said, I may have missed a few in the cities of northern Spain since there seemed to be one on every block.

As a preschooler I used the cry room at Saint Ann's Church in Butte, Montana, for its intended purpose, crying. I blubbered inconsolably because I was imprisoned in a glassed-in room at the far end of the church from the tabernacle. It was completely unfair that others got to be closer to Jesus.

That yearning to be close to Jesus prompted me after Mass one Sunday to approach an old wooden tabernacle stored in a dark, curtained niche at Saint Ann's. This was my chance to see Jesus up close and personal. Trembling like the Lion about to encounter the great and terrible Wizard of Oz, I stretched my fingers up to the knob, eased open the door, and peeked inside.

It was empty.

Jesus must have moved to the ornate, golden tabernacle above the altar. I had missed my chance to be face-to-face with the Lord. There was only one thing to do—blubber inconsolably.

In junior high I began to reason that this is my one life on earth, and thus, I ought to live it in the best way possible. Perhaps the religious life would be the best way to serve God. Ignatius thought as much. He considered joining the Carthusians upon returning from his pilgrimage to Jerusalem. The notion of joining a religious community in which I, too, could imitate the saints remained in my thoughts and invaded my prayers. During liturgical celebrations I would look around and wonder if others heard the Gospel readings speaking to them as I had.

"Come, follow me."

I kept these notions to myself through school, not wanting others to influence my vocational decisions and not wanting to be labeled a seminarian before my time. After all, what girl wants to date a priest-to-be?

After two years of college and another year working at a television station in Billings, Montana, I awoke one morning with the question springing to consciousness, "Is it time, Lord?" I can relate to Ignatius's perception of God treating him like a schoolmaster treats a young pupil. Like a good teacher, God drew out of me the question that it would never occur to me to ask if I didn't already know the answer.

"OK, I get it. It *is* time to look into religious life."

Naturally, with my upbringing steeped in Benedictine tradition, I thought of the monastic life first. After introductory e-mail exchanges with the vocational director at Saint John's Abbey in Collegeville, Minnesota, I accepted his invitation to come for a visit. A couple days later I showed up, with a Santa-size duffle filled with clothing and other essentials, ready to enter the monastery.

Apparently, with over 1,500 years of history, monks like to take things a bit more slowly. The vocational director tried to apply the brakes.

"We are going to need your birth certificate."

"Here it is."

"We also need your baptismal certificate."

"Here it is."

I thought I was ready. The vocational director was clearly not as sure.

For a week I slept in a private room in the cloister, ate in the refectory, worked in several ministries, and prayed in choir with the monks. All that time I pleaded to God to make me feel at home, make me feel at peace. It eventually occurred to me that, if the monastic life was right for me, then I would not have to be praying so hard for God to make it right.

After leaving Saint John's I went to Milwaukee to meet with the Jesuit novice director there. This wise and learned Jesuit was responsible for leading fledgling Jesuits, "novices," through their first two years of formation in the Wisconsin Province. He handed me a copy of the *Autobiography of Saint Ignatius* and a thick book chronicling the history of the Society, both of which I read with considerable interest back on the prairie of Montana.

Ignatius wanted his companions to be men of great, holy, and authentic desires. In one of his letters, he wrote, "They should endeavor to conceive great resolves and elicit equally great desires to be true and faithful servants of God."[6] Early in my Jesuit formation, I wasn't surprised, therefore, when my spiritual director asked me, "What do you most desire?"

"I want to be a saint."

That surprised him. Apparently it is not something he was accustomed to hearing. I tried to explain.

"If I were a comedian, I'd want to be a headliner."

In hindsight I might have come up with a better analogy. I persisted.

"If I were a football player, I'd aspire to be a quarterback. So, as a vowed religious, one whose life is dedicated to the pursuit of holiness, it makes sense to desire sanctification."

Injecting a dose of humility into the conversation, my sage spiritual guide noted that I would have to, in fact, die first. That inconvenience aside, Jesuits have a pretty good track record of being canonized. And so I figured that my odds, although slim, were not impossible.

OK, so maybe it was not *sainthood* I desired. Rather, my authentic desire was, and continues to be, to imitate the saints in living a life of holiness. Ignatius desired as much. "The saints were of the same frame as I. Why should I not do as they have done?"[7]

My desire for holiness led me to read Ruth Burrow's *Guidelines for Mystical Prayer* three times.[8] With each reading I became more frustrated, even depressed. I finally understood that there are no rules, no guidelines, which, if I can only "get right," will advance my peg along the cribbage board of spiritual life. Union with God, and all of its approximations, comes from God alone. It is pure gift, pure grace. That is Burrow's point, of course.

So I am no longer trying to figure out how to achieve mystical union of my own accord. Rather, I am content to simply—and more humbly—keep company with God.

That being said, I appreciate the contemplative moments in my life in which I imagine being in the physical presence of God. What I cherish most about these moments is the sense of utter peace and contentment. Face-to-face with God, there is nothing I need or even want. There is nothing to say or do. I simply rest in the embrace of the Beloved.

While a Jesuit seminarian, I studied philosophy, worked in three hospitals, taught high school, and was the program director at a Catholic radio station in Nome, Alaska. Then, when it came time to write a letter requesting to go on to theology studies, I was surprised to find a lack of desire for ordination. During two years of arduous discernment, I discovered that my truest and most consistent desire was for a family.

I left the Jesuits and worked at a Catholic hospital in Billings, first as a chaplain and then as the director of Spiritual Care. In 1996, I married Evie, a nurse and mother of three children. Attending to my marriage and family then became my primary vocation.

Evie has made two private, directed retreats since we started keeping company eighteen years ago in our loving, devoted, sacramental marriage. These have been incredibly grace-filled experiences in her life. And envy has turned me green enough to make Shrek look pale. *Make a spiritual retreat* tops my list of resolutions every year, right above *get in shape*. Then the months pass without either one happening.

Evie and I came close a few years ago—to making a retreat, that is. We booked a five-day retreat with the Benedictine Sisters in Winnipeg but cancelled to attend to my ailing father. I miss the annual eight-day silent retreats that were such an important part of my life as a Jesuit seminarian. And so I was eager for the Camino de Santiago to be a time of retreat, a spiritual retreat on foot.

The idea of the Camino came from our adult daughter. At first she thought that she would do it on her own. Then Evie became interested in making the journey with her. Books with *Camino* in their titles began piling up on Evie's nightstand. I was happy that this was to be a mother-daughter venture. For me, a modern-day *pilgrimage* conjured up images of gray-haired religious zealots traveling in crowded buses to remote locations to place plastic flowers and lighted votive candles (in painted glass holders) at the foot of statues.

Our daughter's acceptance of a new nursing position necessitated the postponement of her Camino plans. Then, a sabbatical leave became a possibility for me.

A sabbatical, the root of which is *Sabbath*, or *Shabbat* in Hebrew, is a time, not just for rest, but for keeping company. Sabbath keeping is company keeping. On the seventh day, God kept company with all that he had just created. And God saw that it was good—that is, worthy of his attention, worthy of his intimate involvement.

How do we let someone know the goodness we see in them? How do we let someone know that they are truly loved? We spend time with them. We keep company with them. More importantly, though, we give them our undivided attention. On that first day of rest, God's mind was not distracted with regrets about creating mosquitoes and poison ivy. No, God was fully attuned to the woman and man, taking absolute delight in their company.

That is what I wanted from my sabbatical. That is what I prayed for—a sabbatical pilgrimage, the primary purpose of which was to adopt this Sabbath stance of attentiveness, attunement, involvement, and intimacy, inspired by the example of Saint Ignatius.

As I began reading my way through the books on Evie's nightstand, I became more interested in the Camino de Santiago de Compostela. The notion of praying on my feet was appealing.

Jesus invited us to take a walk with him. He invited us to step away, quite literally, from our everyday lives filled with responsibilities and distractions. He did this simply for the sake of keeping company with us. And Jesus invited others along to keep us company as well, including Saint Ignatius of Loyola.

TWO
The Camino Within

My mother often observed, "You're just like your father." It was not always a compliment, yet I always took it as such. One trait I inherited from my father was his "watch and learn" method of imparting knowledge.

Do you want to learn how to change a flat tire? Well, watch me. Do you want to learn how to make a workbench? Watch me. No need for any mumbo-jumbo narration or step-by-step instruction. My mother, a teacher by both profession and predilection, never fully appreciated the merits of this follow-along-if-you-can technique.

My dear mother's contrariness aside, the credit for any insights gained from this book will be yours, the reader, having "watched and learned" while I change a tire. However, I will do you one better than my father might have, by suggesting a few things to keep your eyes on as you turn the pages.

The context and setting for much of this book is the Camino de Santiago. Yet it is not a Camino chronicle or travelogue. It isn't a guidebook. Rather, this book is simply about walking as a way of keeping company—in our case with Jesus, Saint Ignatius Loyola, other saints, Mary, each other, our fellow pilgrims, and the locals who offered us kind and gracious hospitality along the way. Perhaps most importantly, this book is about keeping company with ourselves. The real "camino" is always within.

My first steady, if diminutive, paychecks came from a television station in Billings, Montana, in the early 1980s. As a copywriter I learned that the key to writing a successful commercial is to convince the audience that they have a problem, which the client's product or service will solve—for just $19.95.

I have noticed that books about personal and spiritual enrichment often follow a similar format. The first chapters are devoted to telling us that we have a problem. We are overworked, overstressed, overweight, and more than likely, over budget. A lack of time gets blamed for most of these modern ills. Who has time for the gym? Who has time to cook a sensible meal? Who has time for a spiritual retreat?

This is the section of books that I usually skim or skip altogether. We've heard it all before. We lament the busyness of our lives yet never seem able to do anything about it, either individually or as a society. Maybe, just maybe, it is not busyness that we abhor but idleness. Some credible research suggests that we actually like to be busy and that people who are busy are happier than people who are idle.[8]

I must be one of them. I like to be doing something. And I pray more easily when I am moving. This trait got me into trouble on my second day with the Jesuits.

The novice director confronted me for watering the garden at a time when I was supposed to be praying, presumably in my room or in the chapel. The mindless activity of sprinkling water on seedlings seemed a perfectly natural way for me to tune in to God's presence and simply bask in it. But I was not about to argue the point with the one who held my future as a vowed religious in his hands.

My wife and I have tried to create a prayer space in our loft condominium. In that space you will find a crucifix, Bible, candles, overstuffed pillows, a tabletop fountain, and an antique rocking chair. What you are unlikely to find there is either Evie or me. We are much more likely to go for a walk, even in the middle of Fargo's subzero winters, than to sit in a lotus position frustrated because we cannot get our minds to empty of distractions.

Activities that require little or no concentration, such as strolling along a forest path or watering the lawn with a garden hose, help focus my mind in prayer better than sitting still with my eyes closed. Perhaps this is true for you as well. If so, I invite you to take a reflective, prayerful walk.

You do not have to wade through any how-to manuals. I have yet to see a *Prayerful Walking for Dummies* book at Barnes and Noble. There is no class to take. There is nothing to learn. The multistep process can be summarized simply: take multiple steps.

Walking is something you already do every day. And you already have the necessary equipment, whether it is a comfortable pair of sneakers, a wheelchair, or lacking complete mobility, your imagination, which is the best equipment of all.

Walking has a long history as a spiritual practice. Many of the great religious founders, such as Saint Ignatius of Loyola, undertook pilgrimages and had conversion experiences in the process. And, like Ignatius, they often had to resist the obstructions of civic and religious authorities, even family, along the way.

Yet walking as a spiritual practice is not reserved for the holiest among us. For ages people like you and me have stomped through forests, along beaches, and across mountains simply to marvel at God's beauty and grandeur in nature. Some walk the labyrinths, stations of the cross, and nature paths fanning out from retreat centers, grottos, and monasteries. Some make pilgrimages to the Holy Land, Rome, Santiago, Mecca, Canterbury Cathedral, and other places considered sacred by the followers of the world's great religions. And some simply toddle around their backyards, down the block, or along a local greenway trail having accepted Jesus's invitation to take a walk with him, to keep company with him. Diane Keaggy, writing about my pilgrimage experiences for the *Catholic Health World*, called these *one-mile sabbaticals*.[9] I wish I had thought of that.

This is the kind of walk that really is not about walking. Rather, freed from the distractions of home, classroom, or workplace, it is about listening, being fully attentive, to God and perhaps to another whom God has sent to companion you. Time passes and distances are covered without care, or even notice, because you are so fully attuned to the Other. These are what the renowned philosopher Martin Buber might refer to as *I-Thou* kind of walks.

When we want to become better acquainted with someone, whether for friendship, romance, or even business, we often take a walk together. It is a way of separating ourselves from the herd, so to speak. Romance movies often have a walk scene that takes place on a beach, along the Chicago River, in Central Park, or any number of other settings. Actually, the setting does not matter, at least to the characters, because they are so absorbed in each other.

The scene begins with small talk that includes plenty of giggle-inducing one-liners, especially if Owen Wilson is in the movie. As the couple becomes more comfortable with each other, they begin to reveal more about themselves. They share their hopes and dreams, and perhaps some of their disappointments and failures. Eventually we see the couple strolling silently hand in hand. Although they are no longer chatting, they are still communicating, perhaps even more profoundly than before.

A walk through a city park in Billings turned similarly romantic on one of my first dates with Evie. As she slipped her hand in mine, I felt an exhilarating sense of oneness, communion.

That is a bit of revisionist history, actually. I was, at least momentarily, terrified. Has our relationship suddenly turned romantic? Am I ready for this? Then it occurred to me that Evie's warm, supple hand felt mighty good entwined with mine. "Be quiet," inner voice.

Thankfully, most of the walks I have taken with others have been for the sake of friendship, romance, or simply keeping company. Yet I am also familiar with another kind of walk. It usually begins with, "There's something I'd like to talk with you about. Let's take a walk."

Am I in trouble? Does she have some bad news?

All I know at this point is, first, the "something" is serious and weighty enough to interrupt a rerun of *House*. And, second, she wants my undivided attention. I am being asked to walk with her in order to be free of distractions, not the least of which is our surround-sound, large-screen home theater system. And so I set down the remote, lace up my sneakers, and we head out the door.

Have you ever been invited on such a walk? So, were you in trouble?

Seriously, this is not the kind of walk you do for your health, although, speaking from experience, accepting the invitation does have well-being benefits. By agreeing to the walk, you are demonstrating your commitment to the relationship by literally stepping out of your comfort zone in order to air differences, gain understanding, and hopefully, come to reconciliation. Admittedly, sometimes you just go around and around—both the block and the issues.

This book is about walking simply as a way of keeping company. The walking is no more purposeful than that. It is not a technique or method. It is not a project. It is not something to practice in order to "get right." Walking is simply a means to an end, which is basking in the presence, first and foremost, of Jesus Christ. Thus it pertains to the agenda-free walks of friendship more than to the intentional walks of conflict resolution.

That being said, if you are angry at God, taking a walk is an excellent way to, quite literally, air out your feelings. Attach a

Bluetooth headset to your ear and you can even yell and shake your fist in the air without passersby thinking you are completely nuts. And if you ever hear God saying, perhaps through the voice of your conscience—not your Bluetooth—"There's something I'd like to talk with you about. Let's take a walk," then by all means lace up your sneakers and head out the door.

In *The Four Loves*, C. S. Lewis observes that romantic lovers are usually facing each another, completely absorbed in one another and in their relationship.[10] They talk constantly about their love. He contrasts this with friends who are side-by-side, facing the world together. They talk, not about their friendship, but about their common interests.

Taking a walk with another is most often a side-by-side activity. It is the pastime of friends who are simply keeping company with each other. Side-by-side, as opposed to face-to-face, is a stance of openness toward other people and to whatever surrounds you—the neighborhood, the park, the meadow, the Camino. And because walking is movement, usually outdoors, it is a stance of openness to possibilities, discovery, and change.

Often when "facing" Jesus, with my eyes closed and head bowed, I am like the lover who is focused on the relationship.

Am I praying in the right way? Am I spending enough time in prayer? Am I in good stead with the Almighty?

Yet, when I imagine Jesus at my side as I walk, I am much more at ease, at peace. It could be the increased blood, glucose, and oxygen flowing to my brain. It could be the rhythmic motion. Whatever the cause, walking has that relaxing effect. It helps me clear my mind, forget about myself, and simply enjoy keeping company with the Lord.

With Jesus as my walking companion, I often experience a sense of inner peace, consolation, and love. You will, too. These are moments of grace and blessing. Yet they should not be sought or expected. Remember that you are walking with your Friend, just to be in each other's company. Any attempt to conjure up or merit such gifts just gets in the way of a good walk.

So, would you like to take a restful, peaceful Sabbath walk?

THREE

Bread Fellows and Bedbugs

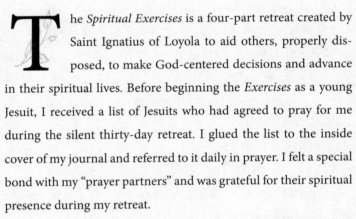

The *Spiritual Exercises* is a four-part retreat created by Saint Ignatius of Loyola to aid others, properly disposed, to make God-centered decisions and advance in their spiritual lives. Before beginning the *Exercises* as a young Jesuit, I received a list of Jesuits who had agreed to pray for me during the silent thirty-day retreat. I glued the list to the inside cover of my journal and referred to it daily in prayer. I felt a special bond with my "prayer partners" and was grateful for their spiritual presence during my retreat.

So I renewed this practice in preparation for the Camino by listing on the inside cover of my notebook those whom I wanted to companion us on the pilgrimage retreat. The list included those whom I am privileged to have as family and friends in this world. It also named Jesus, Mary, Saint Ignatius Loyola, Saint James the Apostle, and others among the saints of heaven, such as my deceased mother and brother.

Every so often Evie claims to hear my mother laughing from beyond the grave. These occurrences happened more frequently on the Camino, perhaps because it was such a spiritually charged time. More likely, though, it was because our follies and trifling concerns must have seemed pretty hilarious to someone with a 90,000-foot perspective.

Along with my chortling mother, I wanted to share the Camino experience with my younger brother. Growing up together I hated to share anything with the obnoxious, competitive creep. But then we did grow up and, as so often happens, became best friends.

Almost every workday Adam and I sent each other short e-mails, his from an office on the 104th floor of the World Trade Center in New York City. Regardless of the content of our messages, the subject lines always referenced Jack Daniel's. On the morning of September 11, 2001, Adam's message was cryptically entitled, "JDJDJackJDJDDanielsJDJD." In it Adam noted that the account he was in the office early to work on that day "will be the end of me." That fateful morning my brother and best friend, J. Adam Larson, became one of the casualties of the horrific terrorist attack on our country.

Ten years later, I continue to be consoled by words of Saint Ignatius, who considered all of life on earth a pilgrimage, with heaven as its destination:

> "If we had our fatherland and true peace in our sojourn in this world, it would be a great loss to us when persons or things which gave us so much happiness are taken away. But being as we are pilgrims on this earth, with our lasting city in the kingdom of heaven, we should not consider it a

great loss when those whom we love in our Lord depart a little before us, for we shall follow them before long to the place where Christ our Lord and Redeemer has prepared for us a most happy dwelling in His bliss."[11]

Believing that, when my pilgrimage on earth comes to an end, I will be reunited with Adam, my mother, and other loved ones gives me a sense of peace about death. I perceive death to be a passageway that will, please merciful God, reunite me with those with whom I wish to keep company for all eternity.

That being said, I have no wish to advance the date of my demise. As confessed in the creed every Sunday, I believe in the communion of saints, which means that I do not have to wait until death to enjoy their spiritual presence. This doesn't make me a spiritualist. I have never participated in a séance in hopes of gaining some insider information about the afterlife. I simply experience, however mysteriously, the loving companionship of saints in prayer. And, since I like to pray while I walk, I just hope they are keeping up while we are keeping company.

Somewhere over Newfoundland on our nine-hour flight to Paris, I lifted and quaffed a shot of Jack "to Adam," present with us in spirit in the here and now. And I did the same in Santiago in glad celebration of his companionship on the 500-mile pilgrimage.

After clearing customs, we made our way through the massive Charles de Gaulle Airport to the train station below, where we were soon on our way to Bayonne, a charming city in northwestern France, for our first night in Europe.

Right from the start, people went out of their way to be kind and helpful. Our journals are replete with entries such as, "We are astonished by the friendliness and helpfulness of people." And, in addition to being considerate, most were incredibly patient with our rudimentary, often incorrect, French and Spanish. One such instance occurred that afternoon in Bayonne, which is about 95 kilometers from Ignatius's hometown. Bayonne was quite familiar to the Saint. It was not to us.

We had reservations at the riverfront Hotel Loutau. If only we could find it.

Searching on the wrong side of the river led us to evening Mass in the impressive Gothic cathedral but didn't get us any closer to our lodging. After Mass we asked two stately women and a gentleman to point us in the direction of our hotel. Instead, the venerable trio clasped our hands and strolled leisurely with us down the street and over the bridge to the hotel, serenading us in lilting French along the way.

The rustic, pilgrim-packed train we took from Bayonne the next morning clattered its way uphill to Saint-Jean-Pied-De-Port, "Saint John at the foot of the pass," in Pyrenean French. We arrived too early in the day to check in to our room. So we left our packs at the desk of the Hotel Central and went exploring.

First we hiked up the cobbled Rue de la Citadelle to the Pilgrim Friends Office (Les Amis du Chemin de Saint Jacques) to get our *credenciales de peregrinos* or pilgrims' passports. These light cardboard documents that unfold accordion style are rubber stamped with *sellos* along the Camino route. They are used by pilgrims to prove that they have walked or bicycled to Santiago and are thus entitled to a *compostela* or certificate of completion. We also obtained traditional scallop shells that, tied to the back of our packs, marked us as Camino pilgrims.

The scallop shell has long been the *signum peregrinationis* of the Camino de Santiago de Compostela. In addition to actual shells dangling from the knapsacks of pilgrims, stylized shell symbols appear on waist-high cement trail markers, road signs, and buildings to guide pilgrims along the Way to Santiago. Scallop shells often decorate albergues, houses, and gardens along the medieval pilgrimage route as well.

Before leaving the pilgrim office we gave 100 euros to the Confraternity of Saint James that staffs it. Later we came to regret, not the donation, but the diminishment of our cash.

More about that later.

Next we took a self-guided tour of the adjoining thirteenth-century Prison of the Bishops, *La Maison des Evêques*, a three-story stone building that is now a museum housing pilgrim clothing and artifacts.

A typical medieval pilgrim cot, with a shabby fragment of sheep skin for covering, made us appreciate our standard double beds (*camas matrimoniales*) in Spain, even with the one long pillow that always migrated toward Evie's side of the bed.

While inside a bleak, claustrophobic cell of the historic prison, I envisioned Saint Ignatius's imprisonments at the hands of the Spanish Inquisition. The first instance occurred while he was at the University of Alcala and the second after he had moved to the University of Salamanca. In both cases, officials questioned Ignatius's competence and authority to teach the truths of the faith, as he often did using his *Spiritual Exercises*. Although no fault was found with his teachings, Ignatius once again took to the road to further his studies, this time to Paris.

After stowing our backpacks in our room, we were fortunate enough to get a table on the outdoor terrace of the hotel's restaurant, where we watched large trout congregating in the diaphanous Nive River below. For lunch we ordered a bottle of chilled rosé and, what else, fresh trout.

That evening we went to Mass at the fourteenth-century Church of Our Lady at the End of the Bridge, *Notre Dame du Bout du Pont*, followed immediately by a pilgrim blessing. The priest invited pilgrims to the front of the church, asked each of us where we were from, and addressed as many as possible in our native language. Then he blessed us, reciting an ancient prayer of blessing:

Oh God, you who took up your servant Abraham from the city of Ur of the Chaldeans, watching over him in all his wanderings. You who were the guide of the Hebrew people in the desert, we ask that you deign to take care of these your servants who, for love of your name, make a pilgrimage to Compostela. Be a companion for them along the path, a guide at crossroads, strength in their weariness, defense before dangers, shelter on the way, shade against the heat, light in the darkness, a comforter in their discouragements, and firmness in their intentions, in order that, through your guidance, they might arrive unscathed at the end of their journey and, enriched with graces and virtues, they might return safely to their homes, which now lament their absence, filled with salutary and lasting joy. Through Jesus Christ Your Son, Who lives and reigns with You, in the unity of the Holy Spirit, one God, for ever and ever. Amen.

The good priest concluded the blessing by invoking the patronage of Our Lady upon our pilgrimage to Santiago. This was a profoundly moving experience, one that brought us to tears.

Such blessings were frequent occurrences after evening liturgies along the Camino. I would not fault a pastor who came to regard these nightly blessing services as routine and tiresome. Yet the personal affect and solemnity with which most of the priests blessed the pilgrims astonished me. It gave me a deeper appreciation for why Ignatius wanted to be a priest and why he founded a sacerdotal order.

After a night of very little sleep, Evie and I were ready for a hearty breakfast to fortify our bodies for the hike up the Pyrenees. Our hotel's dining room server brought us each a plate of sliced bread, which we nibbled on while waiting for our breakfasts to arrive. After some time it dawned on us that the bread *was* breakfast. In fact, bread (*pan* in Spanish) became a staple of every meal on the Camino.

We paused below the *Porte Notre Dame* arch on the way out of town to ask for Mary's protection on our journey and to give thanks for her presence with us. Countless pilgrims have done, and continue to do, the same, thus gaining a sense of companionship with a Mother who nurtures, heals, protects, and defends.

Thereafter we began each day of the pilgrimage by inviting Mary to keep company with us in spirit. It was our custom to stand together on the Camino trail, hold hands, bow our heads and pray, always concluding with the words: "Our Lady of the Way, pray for us. Mother of God, pray for our family."

෴

Many pilgrims make the twenty-eight-kilometer trek over the Pyrenees from Saint-Jean-Pied-De-Port to Roncesvalles in one day. Evie and I decided to do it in two, staying overnight at Orisson, a pilgrim hostel perched on a steep slope of mountain pastureland. This was a good decision for a number of reasons, not the least of which was the sense of camaraderie established with other pilgrims the first day on the Camino.

That evening Joan and Louise welcomed us to join them at their end of a long table in the communal dining room of the albergue. Language salad, tossed and dressed from many lands, filled the room. However, we had no difficulty conversing in English with Louise and Joan, both from Canada, albeit French-speaking Quebec.

We served each other family-style the hearty meal of soup, lamb, beans, and cake while talking about our reasons for being on the Camino. Joan said that she was not there to find God. She knows God is present everywhere. Rather she was on the Camino to simply relish the divine presence, and be affected by it, along the Way of Saint James. Our primary reason for undertaking the pilgrimage was much the same. We wanted to keep company with Jesus on a sacred journey.

Even though we had donned our hiking clothes and backpacks the day before, and had already walked the first eight kilometers of our Camino journey, it was not until that evening that we became pilgrims. Our identities as pilgrims emerged out of the breaking of bread with other pilgrims. It happened through the unconscious formation of a community, a community of pilgrims. We had become *companions*, literally "bread fellows."

A few days later we met up with Louise and Joan again. While staying overnight at a hostel—one that Evie and I had fortunately passed by—Louise had gotten eighty-five bedbug bites that swelled to cover her entire body. Her miserable experience prompted Evie and me to stay in nicer hostels and in hotels as often as possible after that.

In his *Spiritual Exercises*, Ignatius instructs exercitants (those making the *Exercises*) to ask for the graces they desire. The first grace we asked for was for the pilgrimage to offer opportunities for Evie and me to deepen our intimacy through greater attentiveness to each other and to the spiritual dimensions of our relationship. It did not take long for that attentiveness to be put to the test. I failed.

It was late morning on the second day. Evie and I had wound our way up the French side of the Pyrenees following a narrow, asphalt road. The guidebooks warned that this cumulative ascent of 4,500 feet is one of the most difficult parts of the Camino. Even though we weren't particularly well conditioned for such a

Bread Fellows and Bedbugs

49

strenuous climb, we felt good. We felt strong. And we felt close to each other in accomplishing it together. In that setting it was easy to imagine Julie Andrews, arms outstretched, singing atop any one of the high, grassy mountaintops surrounding us, "The Sound of Music" resounding through the valleys below.

Evie interrupted my bellowing "The hills are alive with the sound of music" by pointing to a hand-painted arrow sign.

The crude wooden sign seemed to indicate that the way to Roncesvalles leaves the asphalt road and follows an erosion-obscured path through a gap in the ridge above. None of the yellow arrows or scallop shell symbols we had already come to rely upon as distinct way-markings of the Camino could be seen.

I hastily dismissed the sign—and Evie's suggestion that we heed it—believing that it was either inauthentic or that it indicated an alternative way over the top, suitable only for the sheep that grazed along its sixty-degree slope. Besides, we could see a pilgrim couple on the road ahead.

Evie and I continued walking another couple of miles, becoming increasingly concerned as the road descended in the direction of a distant town that was not on our Camino map. She feigned disinterest as I tried to divert attention away from her anxious mind and swollen feet: "Noah walked with God. And, just think, he had enough energy at the end of the day to build himself an ark. But that was nothing compared to his great granddaddy, Enoch. He walked with God for *three hundred years*."

Mercifully, for us both, my schooling Evie in biblical minutiae was forestalled by the approach of a small white pickup. We waved the driver to a stop and then pointed up and down the road repeating, "Camino?" "Camino?" Censoriously shaking his head, the Frenchman pointed in the direction from whence we had come.

I blame Robert Fulghum for not including "follow directions" in his book *All I Really Need to Know I Learned in Kindergarten*.[12] Although I must admit that my reading finger would have gone right past that bit of advice on its way down the list to "take a nap every afternoon."

Before retracing our steps, Evie and I agreed that, in continuing our pilgrimage, we would pause and consider each other's way-finding perspectives, especially whenever they differed. Sticking to that agreement kept us from making several wrong turns on the Camino. And, even when we did make wrong turns, we did it with one mind.

After adding at least four extra miles to our hike, we returned to the place where the Camino leaves the road. A bit chagrined, yet happy to be on the right trail again, we followed several pilgrims making their way up the narrow path leading to the summit and the border with Spain.

FOUR

Sister Ass Needs to Be Fed

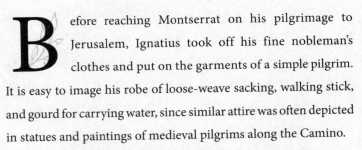

Before reaching Montserrat on his pilgrimage to Jerusalem, Ignatius took off his fine nobleman's clothes and put on the garments of a simple pilgrim. It is easy to image his robe of loose-weave sacking, walking stick, and gourd for carrying water, since similar attire was often depicted in statues and paintings of medieval pilgrims along the Camino.

I have long felt for the poor beneficiary of Ignatius's finery, since he was accused of having stolen the clothes.

Similarly, Evie and I left our travel clothes in our first hotel room, believing that they would be given to someone in need, before putting on our modern pilgrim attire. Thankfully, no one came running after us to inquire if our clothes had been stolen by some unfortunates back in Saint-Jean-Pied-de-Port.

We had heeded the advice of the Camino bloggers and guidebooks in limiting the weight of our packs to less than twenty pounds. That meant carrying only one set of extra clothes.

After checking into the charming La Posada Hotel in Roncesvalles, we washed everything we had been wearing in the bathtub. Thus began our routine of hand-washing our hiking apparel as soon as we checked into the hostels and hotels in order to have a chance of them drying before morning.

Much later in our pilgrimage, I realized that walking poles make serviceable clotheslines when braced between inward-opening windows. Until that point, however, we hand-wrung and hung it all from windowsills, balconies, radiators, lamp stands, and even picture frames to dry. Items that did not dry thoroughly, such as wool socks, hung from the back of our packs the next day.

After bathing, we put on our clean set of clothes and headed for the hotel patio to relax and practice our rudimentary Spanish. In the months leading up to our pilgrimage, Evie and I tried to learn as much conversational Spanish as we could in order to interact with native Spaniards, as well as with our fellow foot-travelers from around the world, using Spanish as the *lingua franca* of the Camino. I ordered *dos cervezas* from the bar. Not just *grande*. I wanted *el más grande*—the largest mugs of cold beer—after all, we had just trudged over the Pyrenees.

Before the mugs were completely drained, I went back inside and ordered two more. I imagined myself a stout, barrel-chested German with bulging forearms carrying huge mugs of frothy Oktoberfest beer to my waiting frau. But as I neared our table, I stumbled on the uneven surface of the patio and smashed the thick, glass mugs into those on the table, drenching Evie with liters of beer and covering her with shards of glass. It is not easy to maintain a chivalric, lederhosen-clad ironman persona while hand-washing beer-soaked clothing in a hotel bathtub.

While people-watching on the patio later that afternoon, we saw a blind pilgrim being assisted by another woman, perhaps a sister or dear friend. The scene caused us to reflect on the unfathomable depth of faith it must require to leave all that is familiar and set out on such a momentous trek without the benefit of sight.

We talked about the importance—even with the ability to see—of the familiar, the ordinary, the routine in our lives. We mused about the routines we had already established on the Camino. We reflected on how routines define our lives and, in many ways, our very being. Routines give our existence presence. The importance of this may be in developing spiritually steeped routines that bring depth and meaning to the ordinary.

We did not encounter the blind pilgrim and her companion again on the Camino and so we do not know how far they progressed. Yet we thought about them and prayed for them often.

⌇

While certainly not on the scale with blindness, Evie had her own physical challenges to overcome, mostly having to do with her feet. The bone is enlarged around the joint at the base of her big toes, which turn in toward her second toes. The tissue surrounding these joints often becomes swollen and tender, especially when she walks for any significant distance. The new orthotics in her hiking boots helped alleviate the pain for the first eleven kilometers or so each morning but after that her feet became quite sore. She likened walking the equivalent of a half marathon day after day to giving birth. "When it is done, you do not remember the pain." That realization offered precious little solace, however, when there were still eleven or more kilometers to traverse before easing into a hot, sudsy bath.

While I attended the evening Mass and pilgrim blessing in the great thirteenth-century church of Roncesvalles, Evie relaxed in our hotel room and wrote in her journal. "My feet are killing me. It is difficult to imagine walking again. I nearly cried today but did not want Luke to feel bad. My poor, pathetic feet need R&R."

Evie might have wanted something to think about besides her pain-ridden feet. She might have wanted to enlarge her circle of heavenly companions to whom she could turn for comfort and to fortify her resolve to continue. Or she might have wanted to draw inspiration and strength from the austerities and penances endured by holy women and men. For whatever the reason, as we made our way to Zubiri the next day, Evie wanted to talk about the saints.

Similarly, Ignatius found solace and inspiration in reading about the saints while waiting for his shattered leg to heal. The debilitating injury was the result of being struck by a cannonball during a battle in defense of the Castle of Pamplona in 1521. After recovering his ability to walk, Ignatius limped his way from Loyola to Montserrat and then to Manresa, sometimes hobbling along with one foot shod and the other bare and bleeding. Undoubtedly that was just one of many times hiking long distances was a grueling ordeal for him. So I believe he answered our prayers with great empathy, sending us his comforting spirit.

Saint Francis of Assisi, who often went barefoot even in the depths of winter, is another saint who could commiserate with Evie's pained feet. Francis often referred to his body as "Brother

Ass," believing that it was meant to carry burdens, to be submissive, to eat scantly and coarsely, and to be disciplined when not controlled. On his deathbed, he asked his body for forgiveness for the excessive austerities he had inflicted on it.

Evie referred to her body similarly on the pilgrimage.

"Sister Ass is ready for a rest break."

"Sister Ass needs to be fed."

Also, like Saint Francis, she asked pardon of her feet for what she was putting them through.

Evie accused me of trying to imitate the saints in their long periods of fasting. Ignatius engaged in this ascetic practice in an attempt to rid himself of scruples and the temptation to end his life while in Manresa. My fasting was far less intentional, let alone spiritually motivated.

In the mornings I was eager to begin walking and became impatient waiting to be served toast and tea. In the afternoons I grew tired of the baguette sandwiches, called *bocadillos*, of sliced chorizo and sheep cheese. So I was content to walk each day, averaging thirteen miles, with just a Snickers bar, small Coke, and half of an apple to sustain me.

Evie was not so content.

"Man does not live on bread alone," I declared.

"Perhaps, but woman would like some every once in a while," she retorted.

Later in the pilgrimage, on the outskirts of Atapuerca, we paused long enough to scratch the chin and pat the head of a red roan donkey. That afternoon we purchased an apple as a treat for the gentle beast. By the time we got back to its pasture, only the core remained. Evie rationalized that the burro has plenty to munch on at its feet. While hiking with me, on the other hand, opportunities for nourishment are much fewer and farther between.

Considering the fruit that hung over the trail as being up for grabs, we helped ourselves to apples, grapes, wild plums, and wild blackberries. I noticed that Evie bypassed olive trees though. Unfortunately, that did not clue me in to the fact that, since olives are rock hard and extremely bitter straight from the tree, I should have bypassed them as well.

At times, others on the Camino route took our nutritional needs into their own hands, literally. Before finishing our dessert in the dining room of the Hotel Monaco in Los Arcos, we asked the waiter if we could have sandwiches made to take with us the next day. He suggested that we help ourselves to the breads, sliced meats, and cheeses from the buffet in the morning. So, after eating breakfast the following day, we returned to the counter to begin assembling our sandwiches.

Apparently, that same waiter thought we were too stingy in helping ourselves. He plucked the bread knife from my hand, sawed open two enormous baguettes, and stuffed them with sliced meats, cheeses, tomatoes, and wedges of Spanish omelet (also called *Tortilla de Patata*, or Potato Omelet). We knew that we would never be able to eat the colossal sandwiches and, frankly, were unenthusiastic about packing the extra weight. Nevertheless, we accepted the foil-wrapped hoagies, grateful for our new friend's Dagwood-sized generosity.

Later in life, Ignatius counseled others away from excessive fasting. As superior general, he wrote to Francis Borgia, a professed member of the Society of Jesus: "As for fasts and abstinences, I would advise you to be careful and strengthen your stomach, for our Lord, and your other physical powers, rather than weaken them."[13]

Ambling along the Camino pathways, we became quite attuned to the sights, sounds, and smells of our surroundings. We experienced nature, not as scenery glimpsed as from a car window, but at our feet and all around us. So we treaded lightly. Our awareness of nature reminded me of how Ignatius found God in all things, even in the small and insignificant. Pedro de Ribadeneyra said in his biography of Ignatius: "We saw how even the smallest things make his spirit soar upwards to God, who even in the smallest things is Greatest. At the sight of a plant, a leaf, a flower or a fruit, an insignificant worm or a tiny animal Ignatius could soar free above the heavens and reach through into things which lie beyond the senses."[14]

Following Ignatius's example, we were single-minded in our desire to be truly present, to be in the moment, at every step along the Camino. We literally stopped to smell the roses, as well as to marvel at purple crocuses, red geraniums, purple Bachelor's Buttons, iridescent green beetles, and multicolored butterflies. We even stopped to look at slugs, which came in varying shades of black, brown, and gray.

Evie and I walked together quite easily for the first six to eight kilometers most days of the pilgrimage. After that her pace slowed considerably. I walked several meters ahead simply because it was too difficult for me, as a tall man with a long stride, to adjust to her pace. However, I always remained within sight. I turned around frequently to make certain that I was not getting too far ahead. And I made sure that we were together while crossing highways and walking through villages and cities.

By staying in hotels, we avoided what is referred to as the *refugio mentality* whereby pilgrims race from one place to the next in time to secure a bed. Other middle-aged pilgrims tried to avoid the crowded albergues as well. Cohorts thus formed with people from around the world as we greeted each other frequently, checked into the same hotels, chatted over afternoon beers, and shared evening meals together.

A couple from British Columbia began each of these encounters by repeating, "Those last two kilometers were the longest."

A Belgium man rattled off the short list of typical first and second plate entrees, thus proving that we really didn't need to see the *menú del día*, or the pilgrims' menu.

We all commiserated about our sore feet, sore backs, and sore throats. Caring bonds formed quickly with people we had only recently met and might never see again.

Evie's misery with her feet was compounded by a chest cold, manifested by a "wicked cough," about two weeks into the pilgrimage. Pilgrims in adjoining rooms in the hostels, kept awake through the nights by her cacophonic hacking, undoubtedly had other words to describe it.

"Luke and I stayed at the *Albergue de Peregrinos* last night too."

"I know. Believe me, I know! Now, if you'll excuse me, I need to find a *quiet* place to take a nap."

Wherever hotels or hostels were either full or nonexistent along the Camino, we cocooned ourselves in lightweight sleep sacks on top of twin beds in the albergues. Fortunately, the chattering of our teeth on those cold autumn nights helped drown out the loud revelry of the Italian bicyclists who always seemed to cram themselves into a room next to ours.

We avoided the noisy, smoke-filled cafés as often as possible. Even when the weather was cool and drizzly, we preferred to spend our Coke breaks and late afternoon leisure time sitting around the plastic tables that were outside most bars and restaurants.

In the afternoons we had incredible conversations with each other, with other pilgrims, and with locals over well-earned, cold draft beers and green olives, *aceitunas*, the ubiquitous cocktail snacks of Spain. The profundity of the conversations took me by surprise. Can we really discern what God expects of us and where God is leading us, as Ignatius so confidently asserts? How is the eternal bliss of the saints not affected by their communing with us who still experience sorrow in this life? How can we share the spiritual essence of our pilgrimage with our family and friends? Comparing the depth of such conversations with the plain vanilla of everyday chatter was truly eye-opening. I had assumed that, in the "real" world, we have such weighty discussions often. Not so. Not like this. I resolved to make time for them more routinely back home.

The *plazas mayores* of the cities and villages, usually sandwiched between an imposing church and an overly ornate town hall, or *ayuntamiento*, provided excellent venues from which to observe the routines of the people of northern Spain. These gathering places bustle with people from late afternoon into the night. Children frolicked, often playing tag, while parents chatted between sips from their tiny cups of *café con leche* at outdoor tables. Grandparents, rapturously attentive to their infant grandchildren in carriages, held our gaze and warmed our hearts the most.

Several times elderly people approached us along the Camino and talked at length in Spanish. It did not seem to matter that we could not understand most of what they were saying.

Undoubtedly we missed some sage advice.

One of the first of these encounters happened in a small café at Arre. A Navarran man seated at the counter took charge of ordering lunch for us, which turned out to be tapas of Spanish tortillas, stuffed mushrooms, and anchovies. The gentleman pointed at his cane, thumped it on the floor three times, and then pointed at himself with a proud grin that lit up his face. These actions were repeated several times. Regrettably, I could not figure out what he was trying to tell me. Evie understood. As we carried our eclectic sampling of food to a nearby table she said, "He walked the Camino three times."

Another time the well-dressed wife and friends of a stately Spaniard went into a restaurant where they were about to dine. He stayed outside to talk with me, a weary backpack-toting pilgrim. Even though it was dark and we stood in a drizzly rain, he was eager, almost desperate, to converse. Quickly realizing that I couldn't understand his Spanish, he tried French before turning to English. He wasn't about to give up. Like the gentleman in Arre, he had walked the Camino three times. How fascinating. What were his reasons? At what ages did he make the pilgrimages? Was he alone? Where were his starting points?

I didn't get a chance to ask any of these questions. The gentleman had some of his own. He wanted to hear about my pilgrimage motivations and experiences. It was more than curiosity that compelled him to abandon his dinner party and approach me in the rain. I believe he wanted to renew, in some instinctive and visceral way, the sense of camaraderie one feels in the presence of a fellow pilgrim. We were kindred spirits.

Before embarking on our pilgrimage, I had read about the honor shown to pilgrims on sacred journeys throughout the ages. Numerous monasteries and convents were erected along pilgrimage routes to provide for the physical and spiritual needs of pilgrims. Several confraternities were formed to ensure the safety of pilgrims. And countless individuals, such as Saint Dominic de la Calzada, devoted their entire lives to clearing pathways and building bridges to ease the way for pilgrims.

This reverence is not a thing of the past. For instance, we passed an elderly man who spent his days standing along the Camino trail gifting pilgrims with the weather forecast. Another time, when we asked a young mother for a cup of water, she went into her house and came back with two cold bottles, for which she wouldn't accept payment. The ways in which profound respect continues to be shown pilgrims—without regard to age, appearance, nationality, motivations, etc.—are astonishing, especially in our often cynical and self-absorbed world of today.

Before our leave-taking that dark rainy night, the three-time pilgrim asked if he could bless me on my way. He did so—like a father might bless his son of any age—in the name of the Father, and of the Son, and of the Holy Spirit.

Amen.

FIVE

Mary on the Way

I was magnetized to the churches all along the Camino route. If we had ever become separated in one of the towns, Evie would have simply looked for me in the church.

For example, there was the small church in the village of Zabaldika, about nine kilometers from Pamplona. Even though it was raining and we were weary from hiking along muddy trails, we were enticed to detour from the Camino by a sign that promised "A Pause on the Way."

We trudged up a steep, mud-slicked path to the Church of Saint Stephen, only to find it locked. After knocking on the door of an adjoining house, we were warmly greeted by Sister Pilar, one of the Religious of the Sacred Heart of Jesus, who tends to the church and its many visitors.

The Romanesque church, built of dressed stone, dates from the beginning of the thirteenth century and has not had any major alterations since its construction. The bell tower rises up from the choir end of the church and is supported by it. Typical of Spanish churches, the bells are in two arched windows.

The gracious Sister Pilar led us to the barreled vaulted doorway, framed by three decorated Romanesque arches, and opened the church for us. She then started a recording of Gregorian chant, and gave us copies of *A Reflection for the Way*, *The Beatitudes of the Pilgrim*, and *Our Father*, all printed in English.

A life-sized crucifix welcomed us at the entrance. Beneath the choir loft we discovered a thirteenth-century baptismal font on the left and a spiral staircase leading to the bell tower on the right.

We knelt in silent prayer for a while, and then wrote petitions for our family on lime green Post-Its and stuck them to the wall around an open-armed wooden statue of Christ Crucified, as countless pilgrims had done before us. The holiness of both Sister Pilar and of the sanctuary touched us deeply. Evie felt the Holy Spirit's presence more palpably there than in any of the great cathedrals we visited in northern Spain.

The church's seventeenth-century retablo, a multiniched construction behind the altar that frames sacred statues, is somewhat modest by Spain's standards. That is much of its charm and beauty. At its peak is a powerful image of Mary being assumed into heaven. In the first row of niches are images of other strong and venerable women: Engracia of Zaragoza, Catherine of Alexandria, Mary Magdalene, and Barbara. The second row includes the deacon Stephen (patron of the parish), Saint Michael the Archangel, the apostle Bartholomew, the martyr Sebastian, and Saint Francis of Assisi. And the third row contains John the Baptist, the apostle James as a pilgrim (the second statue of James on the Camino), Bishop Stanislaus from Poland, and John the

Evangelist. The statues are elegantly carved, each with the symbol by which the saints are commonly recognized, such as the Gospel, sword, or a jar of perfume.

Transfixed on these images, Evie reflected on the multitudes of women and men, including Sister Pilar behind her, who have devoted their lives in the service of God throughout the ages.

"I began the Camino expecting to encounter God and found Mary on the way."

Evie's revelation took me by surprise. I knew that as an adult convert to the Catholic Church, she had lingering suspicions about Marian devotions. Her concerns about the difference between worship, reserved for God alone, and the ways Catholics honor Mary had kept her at a distance from the Blessed Virgin Mary. That changed as Evie began to envision Mary as one whom she wished to emulate, as the perfect model for worshiping, not her, but her Son, Jesus.

Plagued with excruciating pain in her feet, an energy-depleting virus, and severe doubts about her ability to continue, Evie needed the tender, comforting love of a mother.

Mary responded, as a mother would, by keeping company with us. Her understanding and sympathetic presence was not distant and ethereal, but proximate and immediate.

Most importantly for Evie, her company was sustaining.

Mary also provided the example of a strong, courageous woman—a pilgrim—who journeyed to a city of Judah in the hill country to visit her cousin Elizabeth with the news that she was to be the mother of God. She traveled from Nazareth to

Bethlehem while in her third trimester of pregnancy. She participated in the yearly pilgrimages to Jerusalem to observe the Feast of the Passover. And she followed her Son around much of Galilee with, like him, nowhere to lay her head.

"If Mary could keep going under all of those harsh and strenuous conditions, perhaps I can, too."

Evie's newfound connection to Mary helped renew my devotion to the mother of God as well. And it added to my sense of walking in the footsteps of Ignatius, since his life and certainly his pilgrimages always had a strong Marian connection.

Iñigo de Loyola often prayed in the Hermitage of Our Lady of Olatz in Azpeitia, the Basque village of northern Spain in which he was born in 1491. He chose the Church of Our Lady of Arantzazu in which to make a private vow of chastity to Our Lady, entrusting himself under her protection and patronage. And Ignatius left money for a statue of Our Lady to be repaired and properly adorned in Navarrete as he set off on his pilgrimage for Jerusalem.

In his prayers and letters, Saint Ignatius often implored the mother of God to intercede with her Son on behalf of others or on behalf of some consideration requiring discernment. Examples are found in his early letters to Agnes Pascual and Isabel Roser, two of his devoted benefactresses. "May it please Our Lady to intercede with her Son for us poor sinners and obtain this grace for us."[15] "May it please the Mother of God to hear my prayer for you."[16]

We, too, asked for Mary's intercession in praying for specific people on our pilgrimage.

While we had no expectation of Marian apparitions, stories of her appearances and intercessions along the Camino de Santiago are so pervasive that anything seemed possible. Some of these accounts were edifying. Others were somewhat amusing.

Here is just a sampling.

Picture a quintessential medieval king and queen's fairytale castle. Such a fortress actually exists in the historic section of Ponferrada, an industrial city in the province of León. Before constructing the magnificent castle in the thirteenth century to protect the pilgrims on their way to Santiago de Compostela, the Knights Templar had to first clear the site of evergreen holm oaks. In the process they found an image of the Virgin with the Child Jesus in her arms in one of the trees. The discovery led to construction of the sixteenth-century Basílica de Nuestra Señora de la Encina (evergreen oak) across the plaza from the Templar castle. It also led to the Virgin being named patroness of the Bierzo region of Spain.

While Evie and I knelt before a crucifix in that Basílica de Nuestra Señora de la Encina, a woman came up to us and whispered in Spanish that the wooden crucifix is very ancient. I tried to indicate that I understood by saying, "Sí, es muy viejo."

"No, no," she responded, "it is not old, it is ancient." OK, I understand—ancient, not just old.

Another legend involving the Blessed Virgin tells of a teenage boy who, along with his pilgrim parents, stayed at an inn in Santo Domingo de la Calzada. The daughter of the owners fell in love with the boy but her affections went unrequited. So, to spite the lad, she hid some of the inn's silverware in his knapsack. The apparent theft was discovered and the boy hanged. Yet he did not die. This was reported to the mayor as he was about to eat supper. The mayor scoffed, "The boy is as alive as the chicken on this plate." Immediately the chicken leapt from his plate and flew out the door. The innocent boy, whose feet had been supported by Saint James and Mary, was then cut down from the gallows and pardoned.

On the outskirts of León, pilgrims arrive at La Virgen del Camino, where another legend states that the Virgin appeared to a shepherd named Alvar Simón in 1506 and asked him to build a shrine on the spot. Today the sanctuary, dedicated to the Patron Saint of León, the Virgin del Camino, has a distinctly modern exterior with huge bronze statues of Mary and the Twelve Apostles against a wall of dark stained glass.

In the tiny Galician hamlet of Leboreiro, the Camino passes by the thirteenth-century Church of Santa María. Yet another Marian legend has it that the villagers discovered a statue of the Virgin in a local fountain, which emitted a glowing light by night and pleasant aroma by day. They removed the statue from the water and placed it in the church. But each night the statue miraculously returned to the fountain. Day after day the villagers brought the statue back to the church. And so it went until the exasperated villagers decided to carve a stone tympanum of the Virgin and dedicate the church in her honor. Ever since, Santa María de Leboreiro has stayed put in the church.

While visiting with an Irish pilgrim outside the Hostel Camino Real in the village of Caldadilla de la Cueza, I heard a contemporary story involving Mary. It began with a sudden and violent squall that capsized a fishing boat off the coast of Ireland some months previous. Watching helplessly as white-capped swells claimed the lives of his mates, one of the Irish fishermen prayed desperately, promising Mary that, if saved, he would make a pilgrimage to the major shrines dedicated to her.

The fisherman-turned-pilgrim was apparently making good on his promise. Just that afternoon, only a few kilometers distant, he had told his fateful story to the Irish pilgrim who told the story to me.

I do not feel the need to play MythBuster in judging the plausibility of any of these stories. I simply appreciate them for contributing to the sense of Mary's enduring presence among the people of Spain and with the pilgrims of the Camino de Santiago.

That being said, I am suspicious of manifestations in which Mary seems to call attention to herself. Stories, like the one in which Mary demands that a shrine be built in her name, are incompatible with the humble woman from Galilee who regarded herself as a servant of the Lord, whose soul magnifies the Lord. During her life on earth, Mary pointed, not to herself, but to her Son, as Christ's first and most perfect disciple. It is inconceivable that her personality, her patterns of behavior, radically changed after her assumption into heaven.

Another image, which I find impossible to reconcile with the mother of God, is that of a warrior woman who engages in violent conquest, helping one people reign victorious over another. This representation of Mary is prevalent in Spain, where it is believed that she aided in the Reconquest, as well as in the conquest of the Spanish New World. Assisting in the slaughter of native peoples in the Americas is not consistent with the woman who is believed to have prophesied of her Redeemer Son: "He has brought down rulers from their thrones but has lifted up the humble" (Lk. 1:52).

It makes sense that early pilgrims would call upon Mary as intercessor, mediator, advocate, comforter, and protector as they undertook the uncertainties of the Camino. Evie and I did as much, even at a time when the pilgrimage route is relatively safe and reliable accommodations are plentiful. It also makes sense that Mary would make her presence known to those who have undertaken the Camino as a spiritual pilgrimage through the ages.

Like so many pilgrims before us, we invited Mary to keep us company, in our minds and in our hearts, on the Camino. We did so, wanting to become better acquainted, not with a plaster statue image but with a flesh-and-blood woman whose life experiences included both rapturous joy and unspeakable suffering. We looked to Mary as a model of humility, simplicity, piety, and trust in our desire to renew our spiritual lives.

SIX

Things to Be Desired

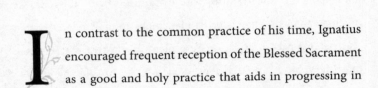

I n contrast to the common practice of his time, Ignatius encouraged frequent reception of the Blessed Sacrament as a good and holy practice that aids in progressing in the virtues of charity, humility, kindness and devotion.[17]

I needed no encouragement. As a Catholic who undertook the pilgrimage for the sake of communing with Jesus, I hungered for daily Communion, *Cuerpo de Cristo*, the body of Christ. A warm shower and clean clothes refreshed my body after long, strenuous hours on the trail. My soul needed refreshment as well. It found nourishment in the Eucharist, the living bread, food for the journey. So I sought out evening liturgies as often as possible on the Camino. A day without Mass seemed incomplete.

I had learned many of the liturgical responses in Spanish. And I could recite the *Padre Nuestro* along with the congregation, as long as it was not said too rapidly. Yet I understood little else. Mostly I was content to allow the mystery of the liturgy to envelope me while praying in thanksgiving for the blessings of the day.

Unfortunately, unless Mass was being celebrated, most of the churches along the Camino were locked. Whenever one was open, we went inside for a few minutes of quiet rest, prayer, and reflection.

In Pamplona, the first major city on our pilgrimage route, Evie and I walked several blocks through the narrow streets in search of Saint Ignatius Church.

It was locked.

While I was taking photographs of its exterior, Evie spotted a bronze statue of the wounded Iñigo de Loyola being attended to by fellow soldiers. The bronze, situated on a grassy patch surrounded by bustling city streets, did little to help me envision the historical setting where a fateful cannonball shattered Saint Ignatius's right leg, unleashing the process that led to his conversion.

Almost two months later, after our walking pilgrimage, Evie and I visited the Tower House, the medieval fortress where the future Saint Ignatius was born. There it helped to see a diorama showing the placement of Saint James's fortress, in defense of which Ignatius was wounded in 1521, within the fortified city of Pamplona.

We did not want anything to detract from our objective of keeping company with Jesus and each other on a walking retreat. We wanted to arrive in Santiago filled with gratitude for the time spent with God rather than with checklists filled with sights visited and camera memory cards filled with photographs taken. Hence, we stopped mostly at places of spiritual significance—churches, convents, and monasteries—along the Camino.

Although the twelfth-century Romanesque Church of Saint Mary of Eunate near Muruzábal certainly qualifies as spiritually significant, I must admit that its curious octagonal shape is what first piqued my interest and captured my imagination. The church is actually a hermitage dedicated to the Virgin Mary. Although its origins remain a mystery, its eight high walls lead many to theorize that it was constructed by the Knights Templar and modeled after the Church of the Holy Sepulchre in Jerusalem.

However, guidebooks are quick to point out that the presence of another military order, the Order of Saint John of Jerusalem or Knights Hospitaller, in this region of Navarre is more historically certain. Questions of construction and patronage aside, early uses of the place include a pilgrim hospital, a funeral chapel, and burial ground.

⤳

Visiting Eunate added three hot, dusty kilometers to our trek between Pamplona and Puente la Reina. When we arrived, we found the holy edifice locked. I was exasperated. Evie took off her boots and stretched out on a bench while I contented myself with slowly circling the building of thick, dressed stone surrounded by a series of arches and a low outer wall.

My disposition gradually improved as I became amused by the sometimes silly, sometimes grotesque heads carved on the exterior corbels of the church. Those who meticulously chiseled the intricate heads undoubtedly intended them as metaphors for life with the good and the evil, the sacred and the profane, the wheat and the weeds existing side by side.

Perhaps moved by Evie's foot-weary demeanor, a caretaker emerged from a nearby hostel and offered to open the church for us. We followed her along the stone path, past the wrought iron gate, and through the arched doorway. Light from the midday sun, softened and diffused by alabaster windows, could not fully dispel the dimness of the chapel's interior.

As my eyes adjusted, they made their way from the floor—with its long, thin stones in a herringbone pattern—up the high white walls to four octagonal and four smaller hexagonal windows in the ribbed ceiling. The opaque windows appeared like stars in the night sky, there to beckon us on to the Field of Stars.

Recalling Eunate's history as a funerary chapel, my mind turned to the pilgrims who never made it to Compostela, whose remains were interred in this sacred place. Far from ghastly or unsettling, the sense of being in the company of those who long ago walked the good walk was calming, comforting. The refreshing coolness, the quiet stillness, the symmetry and simple beauty of the chapel gave me the feeling of being with them in the earth, not in a tomb, but in a baptistery perhaps where one is reborn, where one dies to self and rises with Christ.

"Eternal rest grant unto them, O Lord. And thank you for this restful moment in your company," I prayed.

Eunate has little by way of statuary and adornment. A colorful seated statue of the Madonna and Child behind the altar stands out as the exception. Such images of the Virgin and Child are ubiquitous in the churches of northern Spain. Entire rooms of church and monastery museums are lined with sculptured and pictorial depictions of Mary seated with the Child Jesus on her lap. Some are quite realistic, while others are more stylized, even distorted. Yet all of them gave Evie and me the sense that Mary was presenting her Son to us. She seemed to be assuring us, not only of her presence, but that of her Son, Jesus, on our pilgrimage.

I walked out of the hermitage with renewed vitality convinced that if, like those buried here, we do not make it to the Field of Stars, the spiritual journey will not be made in vain.

⌒

About an hour past Estella, near the Monastery of Nuestra Senora la Real de Irache and the Museo del Vino, is one of the must-stops of the Camino de Santiago. It is a wine fountain, *Fuente del Vino*, which is actually a tap protruding from the side of a building. Weary, sore-footed pilgrims line up to fill their water bottles with the wine, which, while not especially good, is free. And it does provide a modicum of relief from the ever-present weariness and soreness one feels on the journey.

While sampling the wine and taking photographs of each other at the fountain, a middle-aged pilgrim approached us, whom we recognized from our evening together at the Orisson albergue. During group introductions that first night on the Camino, we learned that this Canadian and his gregarious, twenty-something daughter were intending to walk the Camino together. Yet here he was, less than a week into the pilgrimage, by himself. He explained that his daughter had met other pilgrims her age and wanted to go on with them at their faster pace. Unfortunately, the father-daughter bonding adventure he had anticipated was not coming to pass, yet the man seemed at peace with his decision to continue on his own.

We told him of our young adult sons, daughter, and daughter-in-law, who, if they were undertaking the Camino with us, would undoubtedly find it frustrating, if not impossible, to walk at our pace. We also talked about the pilgrimage being a solitary experience, even when the Camino route is crowded with other pilgrims.

After wishing each other a "Buen Camino" and parting company, Evie and I prayed for the man and his daughter. We asked God to bless them with safety and especially with the graces that they each needed most from the experience.

Ignatius the Pilgrim often preferred to walk by himself "since the whole purpose was to have God alone for refuge."[18] Like Ignatius, walking was our time of silent retreat. So we often tried to avoid visiting with others for extended periods while walking.

No matter the number of pilgrims that accompany you, the Camino is a personal journey. And, to the extent that one is making it as a spiritual pilgrimage, it is mostly an interior journey. In this regard, the well-marked route left my mind free to "retreat," to meditate and to pray. There were many times of peace and spiritual consolation.

Times of convalescence and pilgrimage gave Ignatius plenty of time to reflect and pray as well. These reflections gradually led Ignatius to distinguish between the spirits that stirred within him. What is more, he began to understand that some were from God and others from the evil spirit. The latter left him indecisive, disquieted, and discouraged. He referred to this spiritual unease and dryness as desolation.

Thoughts and feelings originating with the Holy Spirit, on the other hand, left him with joy, peace, and profound gratitude.

"The fruit of the Spirit is love, joy, peace, forbearance, kindness, goodness, faithfulness, gentleness and self-control" (Gal. 5:22–23). This Ignatius called consolation.

Distinguishing the spirits that produce consolation from the spirits that bring desolation is the work of discernment. It enables us to understand God's movement in our souls and God's purpose in our lives.

Times of pilgrimage walking and resting gave us plenty of time to pray and reflect as well. And, just as Saint Ignatius wrestled with conflicting thoughts, feelings, and desires, I did too. Thoughts of trust, humility, service, and simplicity of lifestyle left me peaceful, filled with spiritual consolation.

Other thoughts and feelings had the opposite effect. They disquieted my mind and soul along the way to Santiago. "The enemy tries to upset you and to interfere with your service of God and your peace of mind," warns Saint Ignatius.[19]

Indeed, a tiny fork-tongued tempter, perched on my left shoulder, kept trying to get me to turn the pilgrimage retreat into just a hike, a tour, or more insidiously, a race. The little bugger was more successful than I care to admit.

I would be seething because we had to wait for our paltry breakfast of toast and tea. "We could have been on our way an hour ago," my unwelcome shoulder jockey would point out.

I sometimes found myself speeding up as other pilgrims passed us. "Are you going to let them beat you to the next village where they will likely occupy the last available chairs outside the café where you are going to want to take your Coke break?"

And then there were times when I acted like I was on a scavenger hunt, racing to add to my collection of instances and images. "Snap a picture of that Saint James statue before the custodian catches you taking photos in the church."

Most ashamedly, I allowed the demented demon to whisper too freely in my ear as Evie's pace slowed in the afternoons and I became anxious to get to our destination. "Why can't she walk as fast as she did this morning? She's not even trying to catch up."

⤚

Desiderata is Latin for "things to be desired." It is also the title of a prose poem by Max Ehrmann.[20] Two of the famous poem's phrases characterize what I desired from the pilgrimage retreat. First, I wanted to "go placidly amid the noise and haste," and second, I wanted to "avoid loud and aggressive persons." These were more easily accomplished during the first days of the pilgrimage.

There were relatively few pilgrims on the Camino with us from Roncesvalles to Pamplona. Villages, such as Auritzberri-Espinal, seemed devoid of people. It felt like we were on the set of a movie as we walked among the gleaming white, two-story houses accented with red-tile roofs and red geraniums in flower boxes below each window. At any moment I expected to hear "Action!" and then to see people streaming out from behind the picture-perfect facades.

As we progressed toward Santiago de Compostela, the Camino became increasingly congested and, consequently, walking "placidly amid the noise and haste" became more of a challenge.

Two pilgrims stood out as examples of "loud and aggressive persons."

Every word that came out of the mouth of an overbearing pilgrim from the Northwest was as pointed as the tip of her walking stick.

"Speak English?"

"Finished with that?"

And a man from Scotland saved little breath for breathing as he went on and on about himself. During our second encounter I eventually interrupted him, saying to Evie, "We have to go." I still feel remorseful for our abrupt departure, yet such people really were "vexatious to the spirit" on the Camino.

My spirit was vexed the most by a group of teenagers wearing military fatigues outside our hotel in Nájera. They loitered by the bus stop in front, by the open-air market to the side, and most disturbingly, by the walking bridge over the otherwise peaceful Najerilla River to the back of the San Fernando Hotel.

Not quietly, though. The pyro-maniacal youths tossed ear-splitting firecrackers at the feet of passersby and launched directionless missiles in the midst of the crowds. I wondered why the local police did not intervene. I wondered why the hotel management did not try to stop them. And, as the afternoon wore on and my nerves wore out, I wondered why I did not confront the hooligans myself.

While generally supportive of my desire to imitate Saint Ignatius, Evie thought having my legs shattered in a vastly outnumbered battle might be taking things a bit too far. She suggested we visit the historic—and serene—monastery of Santa María la Real instead.

As we were about to leave, we saw the paramilitary thugs filing into the hotel's conference room through a side door, no doubt to plot their next bombings. Now we understood why the management hadn't called the police. These were customers!

The monastery, built in 1032, underwent a number of modifications in the fifteenth century. Its fortress-like exterior contrasts with the ornate beauty of the Cloister of the Knights, so-called because of the numerous nobles buried there. The monastery contains a magnificent Romanesque image of Santa María la Real; the cave where the Virgin appeared to King Don García; the Royal Pantheon with the tombs of thirty monarchs; and the mausoleum of the Dukes of Nájera.

The monastery church, cloister, and tombs of medieval monarchs were remarkable. Yet I was eager to visit a monastery where monks still live, work, and pray.

The next morning, while paying for our breakfast of croissants and tea at the Hotel Fernando, I mentioned to the cashier that my wife and I were about to detour from the Camino to visit San Millán de la Cogolla with its two famous sister monasteries of Suso (the one above) and Yuso (the one below). He offered to call us a taxi. I told him that we are pilgrims (*peregrinos*) and that we intended to walk. Looking at us like we were loco, he said in Spanish, "It is twenty-two kilometers to San Millán!" We nodded knowingly. Then the cashier raised his arm at a forty-five-degree angle indicating the steep incline of the trek ahead of us. Again we nodded. The incredulous cashier just shook his head as he watched us don our backpacks and head for the door.

The ascent was more gradual than what the cashier had forewarned and we had feared. Yet our feet, not to mention our spirits, did not take kindly to walking on the asphalt shoulder of the road all the way up to San Millán de la Cogolla. The approach yielded an impressive view of the Yuso Monastery, nestled in the Cogolla Mountains and surrounded by the small village of San Millán. Yet, at that point, Evie's eyes were too blurred with tears of pain, exhaustion, and discouragement to appreciate the view. She wanted desperately to settle into our hotel room, located in a wing of the monastery, as quickly as possible.

After a rejuvenating bath, glass of sparkling wine, and a siesta, Evie was ready to join me for a tour of the monastery. Highlights included the Gothic cloister, sacristy, Hall of Kings, and the eleventh-century coffer that preserves the relics of Saint Millán and tells the story of his life through figures intricately carved in ivory.

The tour was entirely in Spanish so we understood little of what was being said, including our guide's strict admonition not to take flash photographs of the ancient manuscripts in the scriptorium.

Click. Flash.

Dead silence. Icy scowls from everyone in the room. OK, this I understand. No translation needed.

I could not retreat to the sanctuary of the Church of the Assumption of Our Lady. Unfortunately, it was closed for archeological excavation and much-needed renovation. Nor could I find solace among the Augustinian Recollect friars. The receptionist informed us that we were not allowed to participate in their communal prayers and liturgies, possibly because of some unfortunate incidents with flash photography in the past.

The church reopened four months later to again serve as the parish church of San Millán de la Cogolla. While we were there, however, liturgies were held in a much smaller church tucked in the midst of the village. There we were fortunate to witness a commemoration of the transferring of the remains of San Millán, or Saint Emilianus, which led to the construction of the Monastery of Yuso.

The same ornate box reliquary we had seen in the monastery museum the evening before was carried on a litter on the shoulders of four men. The procession was led by well-choreographed teenager dancers, dressed in traditional Basque costumes, leaping and twirling their way through the village streets.

The Yuso monastery houses the hotel where we stayed. Its much smaller and older twin, Suso, was founded by Saint Millán in the sixth century and was a pilgrimage destination long before the Camino. The charming little monastery began as a group of primitive hermitage caves, to which a church was later added. It is famous for its role in the development of the Spanish language. It was there that Castilian and Basque phrases were discovered next to the Latin text in one of the monastery's early codices, or thick books. The codex, written in the Suso scriptorium in the ninth and tenth centuries by one of the monks, had been preserved in Yuso's library before it was moved to Madrid.

Early on our third day in San Millán, Evie and I hiked the 1.7 kilometers up to the site of the uninhabited monastery. Its doors were locked. No one else was there. So we walked around the exterior of the monastery, examining its Mozarabic construction and wondering what life was like there 1,500 years ago. We peered into caves, cut into the southern slope of the mountain, once occupied by Suso's eremitic monks.

An hour later a tour guide arrived and informed us that we needed to purchase tickets at the Yuso office before we could enter. I explained that we were *peregrinos* who walk everywhere we go—including up and down mountains—but not any more than necessary. I promised to pay for tickets as soon as we returned to the Yuso Monastery. All of this was said in my halting, pigeon Spanish. Weary of her native language being drawn and quartered so mercilessly, she finally put us out of her misery and admitted us.

Once inside the nearly empty church, we took pictures of a stone sarcophagi, tombs of the seven princes of Lara, and the three queens of Navarra. Soundly chastised for doing so, we retreated to the peace and quiet of the entrance porch, or narthex, to savor magnificent views of the surrounding mountains and the village of San Millán below.

After our three-day retreat at the Hostería Monasterio de San Millán de la Cogolla, we were ready to resume our trek toward Santiago. I eagerly arose at 6:00 a.m., long before dusk and the serving of breakfast, so I lay back down until 7:30 a.m. Once back on the road, the eighteen kilometers to Cirueña, where we rejoined the Camino, were covered rather effortlessly. We were happy to be back among fellow scallop-shell-bearing pilgrims. Once again we were in the stream of humanity making its way westward to Santiago. That flow, that current, has an energy of its own that is uplifting and sustaining. Walking with others lightens the journey somehow.

Each day brought new people into our lives, and often into our hearts. Friendships form quickly along the Camino, often without regard to age, gender, income, occupation, nationality, and even last names. At what moment did the scruff-faced retired man from Australia become a mate, one we were delighted to reencounter along the Camino and for whom we prayed often? At what point did the young atheist from the Czech Republic become a friend? The precise moments elude me. Such friendships were not so much *made*. They just seemed to happen. They came as gifts from a God who calls us to be in communion with one another, to keep company with each other on our pilgrimages through life.

The Camino is not about the stunning cathedrals, churches, monasteries, convents, monuments, and other cultural and historic landmarks. More than anything else it is about the people—fellow pilgrims and locals alike—who became our friends, even if just for a day or two. No matter where we hailed from, or what motives brought us to trek the road together, we were profoundly grateful for these friendships.

A Thin Place

We speak familiarly of spiritual things with a few, as one does after dinner, with those who invite us,"[21] Ignatius once said. He was talking about time spent with his companions. Similarly, our casual conversations frequently turned to spiritual matters. And although Evie and I did not consciously seek out spiritual persons for such conversations, as had the Saint, we were naturally drawn to those who were on the Camino for spiritual reasons.

In these interactions I tried to adhere to the wisdom of Ignatius: "Be slow to speak, and only after having first listened quietly, so that you may understand the meaning, leanings and desires of those who speak."[22] However, in truth, my reserve was borne more often out of fatigue than conscious intent or virtue.

Another bit of counsel from Ignatius might apply to a conversation we had with three pilgrims from Ireland over a wee pint or two on the patio of a bar in Atapuerca. Ignatius advised: "Try to be humble by beginning at the bottom and not venturing into lofty subjects unless invited or asked, or discretion should dictate otherwise, taking into consideration time, place, and persons."[23]

We talked about our pilgrimage experiences, our countries, politics, economics, travel, and a host of other subjects. John, unemployed at the time, kept the conversation "humble" with his litany of emphatic declarations liberally salted with adjectives best suited for Irish pubs.

Simon, a chemist, lent his quirky sense of humor to our banter. And Chris, a dairy farmer with an encyclopedic mind, amazed us with his vast knowledge of everything from world history to current affairs. He knows who the secretary of commerce is in the United States. I do not.

After chatting and laughing together for hours, Chris declared, "*This* is the Camino." We all readily agreed. The Camino is not about making it to Santiago de Compostela. It is about enjoying the company of others along the way.

When the time seemed right to "venture into lofty subjects," I posed some questions.

Is the Camino spiritually charged? Is it holy ground?

Or is it more like a blank slate with no inherent meaning, purpose, or grace?

Chris responded by telling us about a book entitled *The Heart of Christianity: Rediscovering a Life of Faith*.[24] In it, Marcus J. Borg lists pilgrimage among the spiritual practices that can be considered "thin places."

The notion, derived from Celtic Christianity, is that there are places where the boundary between God's transcendence and immanence is "very soft, porous, permeable." "Thin places," says Borg, "are places where the veil momentarily lifts, and we behold God . . . all around us and within us."

I believe the Camino de Santiago is one of those "thin places" in our world. Whether or not people set out on the Camino for spiritual reasons, they are somehow affected by the pilgrimage, even in ways that they might not realize until well afterwards. The veil lifts along the Way and the Holy gets through. Grace happens. It is not earned. It is not merited. It is, rather, an undeserved and even unexpected gift. And it is a gift that has been bestowed on pilgrims since the mid-tenth century when Santiago began to take its place with Jerusalem and Rome as a leading pilgrimage destination.

After the pilgrimage, I lamented not having solicited and recorded more stories of interest from pilgrims, such as our mates from Ireland. Trawling minds and hearts for their motivations in undertaking the pilgrimage surely would have yielded many fascinating and inspiring accounts to include in this book.

More likely, it would have led to many lonely days on the trail.

"Hey, where is everyone going? I want to ask you something."

"First, has anyone seen my wife?"

Fortunately, that did not happen. Evie reminded me that the purpose of the pilgrimage was simply to companion holy men and women, of both heaven and earth, on a journey—not to interview them. I imagine that is what heaven is like, being totally present in the eternal moment with others and with God. Heaven is ultimately keeping company. And keeping company now is God's kingdom on earth as it is in heaven.

Not every moment on the Way of Saint James was paradisiacal, of course.

A day's walk from Burgos, well into the Meseta, is Hornillos del Camino, a village of about a hundred people. The town's six-table restaurant filled quickly with pilgrims at 7:30 p.m. The world's worst waitress semifinals must have been taking place that night. A white-uniformed server earned our votes. She shuffled among the tables dispensing hot food and cold gusts to each of the guests. She hissed at me until I realized that she wanted me to take my fork off of my plate. Then she swept away our first-course plates before we had a chance to finish.

That was nothing compared to what she did to a young pilgrim from Mexico.

The pilgrim tried everything she could to be friendly but the waitress treated her all the more disdainfully. The server slopped down a bowl of soup in front of the seated pilgrim and then, while retreating to the kitchen door, caught sight of the pilgrim about to add olive oil to her soup. The server yelled from across the dining room, "That's for salads only!"

The pilgrim responded, "I won't allow you to treat me this rudely."

The server pointed toward the door and bellowed, "If you don't like it, you can leave."

The pilgrim stormed out the door without having eaten anything of her dinner.

All of us in the restaurant grumbled about the server and felt sorry for our fellow pilgrim. An affront to her was an affront to us all. Yet we remained to finish our meals, albeit hastily.

I once read on a motel sign, "If you cannot sleep here, it's your conscience." Well, that night our consciences kept us awake. We should have said something to the server. We should have followed the pilgrim from Mexico out of the restaurant.

Following in the footsteps of Saint Ignatius the Pilgrim meant attending to the physical, as well as the spiritual, needs of others, as he did at a hospital in Manresa. On another occasion, while hiking across the mostly treeless and windblown grain fields of the Meseta between Castrojeriz and Frómista, Evie and I came upon a young pilgrim sitting cross-legged on bare ground beside the Camino trail. When we asked if she was OK, she began to sob, telling us of a sore throat and stomachache. We gave her some ibuprofen and Tums and then reluctantly continued on our way.

We walked about a mile before deciding to return to check on our fellow sojourner from Switzerland. She had not moved.

I strapped her much larger—and much heavier—pack on top of mine. We then walked slowly with her to an albergue, about five kilometers distant. An adaptation of a popular 1969 ballad became my silent mantra along the way: "Her pack ain't heavy, she's my sister."

A couple days later we came across our newfound friend and were happy to learn that, after a day's rest, she had recovered completely.

We dedicated each walking day of the pilgrimage to praying for a person or intention. We prayed for specific blessings for family members, relatives, friends, colleagues, fellow pilgrims, and anyone who had asked for our prayers.

"Help cousin Mark find work that will add meaning and purpose to his life."

"Bless Richard with consolation and peace as he struggles with leukemia."

We also invited whomever we were praying for to walk with us in mind and spirit. Depending upon the number of kilometers walked on a particular day, some got more of a workout than others. Along the way we talked with them about what they might want or need in life: mostly love, peace, and forgiveness. In turn, we asked them to help us continue walking in spite of our aching feet.

Confident in the companionship of Saint Ignatius, Saint James, Saint Luke, and a cadre of other holy men and women, I called upon them to join me in praying for each person as well. Patron saints were especially invited into the circle.

"Saint Matthew, pray for Matt."

"Saint Peter, pray for Pete."

"Saint Athanasius, well . . . you can pray for Pete too."

The day we walked from Frómista to Carrión de los Condes was dedicated to world peace. Ironically, I was not at all peaceful that day. There must be something to the notion that the attitude one projects is the attitude one receives. Café owners, storekeepers, and hotel clerks sensed my mood even before I had a chance not to say "Hola." Their surliness amplified my own.

Even the Camino seemed to turn against me. Spelunking gnats set up base camps in my nose and mouth. And the *senda,* the large-pebbled Camino trail through much of Palencia and León, pounded mercilessly at the soles of my feet.

After arriving in Carrión de los Condes, I was eager to check into our room in the hotel section of the Monasterio de San Zoilo. Separated from the town of Carrión by the river of the same name, the tenth-century monastery was originally named after John the Baptist and then later rededicated to San Zoilo, a martyr from the city of Cordoba. There, in its monastery church, I would surely find the peace that had eluded me throughout the day.

It was not to be, as I tried to pray under the soul-piercing gaze of the corpus on a sidewall crucifix. The Christ figure's dark complexion, head covered with long, black hair—actual human hair—and transfixing eyes combined to create an image that was anything but peaceful.

Spanish crucifixes, like that one, often depict Jesus Christ bloodied, beaten, and obviously suffering. I found them challenging to look at and to reflect upon. That was the intent of the sculptors, of course. The crucifixes were stark reminders of Jesus's ultimate pilgrimage to Jerusalem at a time when I wanted to stay with the image of Jesus, the itinerant preacher, strolling around Galilee proclaiming the Good News of the coming of the kingdom.

Peace was in short supply that night as well.

Around 3:00 a.m. I was roused from my slumber by several loud, distinct thumps. It sounded like someone was banging on the floor just outside our hotel/monastery room door. The noise must be coming from a steam radiator, I supposed. Yet, when I looked out into the hallway, there were no radiators. After returning to bed, the thumping sounds resumed.

Someone in the adjoining room must be making the noise. I went out in the hallway and put my ear to the door of the neighboring room. If there were any occupants inside, they were not stirring. Again, after returning to bed, the dull thuds continued.

Fresh out of possible explanations, I began to wonder if a spectral circator, a monk charged with rousing his somnolent brethren for early morning Matins, was a little too diligent—perhaps a thousand years too diligent—in carrying out his duties.

As we soon learned, according to a centuries-old legend, a blind pilgrim kept vigil through the night before the relics of San Zoilo in the monastery. With the rising of the sun in the morning, the man miraculously regained his eyesight. Now I have a pretty good idea how he remained awake through the night.

Thump, thump, thump.

Besides noises—whatever their source—the peace of my pilgrimage was also disturbed when I accessed e-mails. About halfway along the Camino I used a hotel lobby computer to look through the long list of messages in my office inbox. Although I derive much satisfaction and fulfillment from my work, and am energized in the midst of it, scrolling through e-mails pulled me away from the sanctuary of my retreat. I resolved not to do that again on the pilgrimage. Instead, in this age of e-mail, cell phones, texting, Facebook, Twitter, LinkedIn, and YouTube, the Camino afforded numerous opportunities to experience the incredible effectiveness of good old-fashioned word-of-mouth communication.

In fact, the Camino has long served as a conduit of information. The twelfth-century illuminated *Codex Calixtinus*, the original pilgrim guidebook, notes that "pilgrims carried news through all of Spain." We discovered that news continues to travel along the pilgrimage route with unbelievable speed and efficiency today.

"Are you the couple from Fargo? There is a young pilgrim named Greg, also from Fargo, who is anxious to meet you."

An hour later, while Evie and I were sharing an apple under a shade tree, a young man walked up to us.

"Are you from Fargo?"

"You must be Greg."

As we walked along, Evie, a registered nurse, counseled Greg how to treat the blisters on his sandaled feet. She also advised him what to jettison of the surfeit over-the-counter pain relievers and first-aid supplies in his overladen pack. In turn, Greg lightened our spirits with his contagious energy, enthusiasm, and sense of high adventure.

Another time a fellow pilgrim told us of a woman from Australia whose backpack had been "pinched" outside of a hostel earlier that day. While still seated at an outside table in the Cathedral plaza of León a couple hours later, a woman approached and began conversing with us. I noticed first her Australian accent and second that she was not carrying a pack.

"Was it your backpack that was pinched this morning?"

News must have been just as agile in the 1500s. Aware of this, Saint Ignatius took a more circuitous route to the seaport city of Barcelona in order to avoid being recognized on his pilgrimage to Jerusalem. This brought him to Manresa, where he ended up staying for eleven months.

Thirteen years later, while traveling back to his home region of Spain from Paris, his family had been alerted that Ignatius was in the vicinity, even though he had intended to pass by Azpeitia unannounced. A more colorful account has Ignatius concerned that two armed riders who approached him on a remote mountain road might be bloodthirsty cutthroats. Fortunately, the men turned out to be servants of his brother sent to meet him.

While relaxing outside a café in the village of Hontanas, Evie and I overheard a man talking with another pilgrim as they, too, enjoyed chilled Cokes. The pilgrim mentioned that he is a Catholic priest and a recently retired Navy chaplain. We introduced ourselves.

"I'm Luke and this is my wife, Evie."

"I'm Tom. I've heard quite a bit about you. You're that amazing couple from North Dakota." Father Tom had met our trio of Irish friends the night before. I was curious about how we merited the distinction of "amazing" but didn't ask.

꩜

The pilgrimatic grapevine continued to precede us to a bar crowded with rain-soaked pilgrims in the tiny hamlet of Bercianos del Real Camino. Father Tom had mentioned that another priest was within a day or two of us on the Camino. That morning, as we were making our way from Sahagún to El Burgo Reneros (Town of the Frogs), I was comfortable wearing my lightweight Patagonia T-shirt and rain jacket. But as the rain and chilling wind increased,

I began to worry about hypothermia; I was incredibly grateful for the shelter of the bar.

Intent only on getting warm, I had no desire to talk with anyone. I stared at my cup of hot tea, trying to avoid eye contact with the pilgrims crowded around us. Then, inescapably, I found myself looking directly into the eyes of a kindly, middle-aged pilgrim at an adjacent table. If there is such a thing as a pastoral presence, this man has it.

"Are you Father Steve?"

"Are you Luke?"

Evie and I had incredible conversations with Steve and Tom whenever we met them along the route. One of these centered on the historical contexts for Santiago Matamoros, Saint James the Slayer of Moors. We shared our mutual angst about this personification of the saint, which allegedly began in the ninth century with a battle won by an Iberian king against the Moors with the help of Saint James.

How could images of an apostle, saint, and pilgrim be reconciled with that of a slaughterer of people? Should this latter image even exist in this age of religious tolerance?

Chatting about Saint James led to comparisons with Saint Ignatius Loyola, with their shared histories as soldiers and pilgrims, at least mythically in the case of James. I told Tom and Steve about my desire to keep company with Ignatius and how that led to our pilgrimage.

"How can you be sure that Saint Ignatius is keeping company with you?"

"How can you be confident that, simply because you extended the invitation, it was accepted?"

Father Steve and Father Tom did not ask these questions to sow the proverbial seeds of doubt in us. As well-practiced soul plumbers, they intended to stimulate reflection.

My confidence in Ignatius's companionship came, certainly not out of a sense of my own worthiness to be in the presence of such a great and holy saint, but from Ignatius himself. Saint Ignatius's assurances to others were the source of my confidence that, not only was he keeping company with us, but that his intercessions on our behalf were efficacious.

Ignatius took quite seriously others' requests for his prayers. He wrote in response to one such petition: "As to praying for you and having others do so, that I will undertake very willingly because I desire for you, as I ought, not only every perfection but every consolation as well."[25]

In another letter he tried to comfort a lady with this assurance: "On my part, I shall not cease together with those with me here earnestly to recommend your interests to God our Lord."[26] Thus those who called upon the Saint for prayers while he was alive could be confident in his unfailing and unceasing response.

Ignatius believed that we can rely on those in heaven to assist us as well. "Everywhere we have need of the intercession of friends and saints, and we hope that in the Divine Majesty—His will being now fulfilled—[they] will now be no less a source of help to us than [they] would be if [they] were living among us."[27]

He also believed that the desires and prayers of the deceased "will be more efficacious in the Divine presence."[28] And, while we grieve the fact that they are no longer physically present with us, we should "congratulate ourselves on the supreme blessing and happiness of our brothers who will help us better from heaven than they could have done on earth in all that pertains to God's service."[29] It is inconceivable that Ignatius, who believed so resolutely in the reliability of saints' intercessions while on earth, would turn a blind eye to us from his seat in heaven.

While parting company each time, I would simply say to Tom and Steve, "See you later." They thought it optimistic, perhaps even a bit presumptive, that we would continue to run into each other along a five hundred-mile route. Yet it happened often enough that I simply believed that it could happen again.

⌒

After leaving the cramped bar in Bercianos, we hiked the remaining 7.5 kilometers to El Burgo Reneros. There we found another crowded, smoke-filled bar where we had been told to look for the hostel where we had a room reserved. An old, shrewish woman led us upstairs to Room 13 and unlocked the door with a skeleton key. No kidding.

One guidebook described the accommodations as "shabby and noisy." The author was being kind. The room was dirty and the furnishings in disrepair. The mismatched sheets on the twin beds were threadbare.

Evie has a keen sense of the spirit of places. Her pilgrimage journal is filled with notations such as "this is a place of peace" and "this is a place of warmth." This wasn't such a place. Beyond the obvious physical defects, Evie felt ill at ease just being in the room. She cried inconsolably.

We walked around town trying to find something better than our flophouse room above the raucous bar. Every place was *cupo completo*, completely full.

So, at 3:15, we decided to walk on to Mansilla de las Mulas, twenty kilometers distant. Evie bounded along the trail, motivated by fear of being stranded in the countryside after dark. I struggled to keep pace.

She later recounted how she had called upon Mary to get her through the day. Mary was both a source of comfort and strength. Evie also drew strength from the thought of her brother walking by her side and encouraging her, as one might with a little sister.

We arrived in Mansilla around 8:00 p.m., having hiked in one day what we had intended to do in two, over thirty eight kilometers.

Most pilgrims stay in Mansilla before going on to León. As we walked around in the dark and cold rain, discovering that all of the albergues and hostels were full, we gained a more empathic understanding of how Joseph and Mary, weary of travel and heavy with child, might have felt in trying to find shelter in Bethlehem. It seemed like we were reenacting La Posada.

"Move on. There is no room in this inn."

Finally we found a room above a noisy, smoke-filled bar. The furnishings were Spartan. The twin beds were little more than cots that flipped up when we sat on their ends. Yet the sheets were clean. And we were out of the rain.

*Keeping
Company
with
Saint
Ignatius*

100

Just as Evie and I began our days in prayer, we ended them in prayer as well. Praying by name for our children and grandchildren always came first, followed by our relatives, friends, colleagues, our fellow pilgrims, and others who had requested our prayers on the Camino.

In concluding the pilgrims' blessing after an evening Mass, a parish priest asked the pilgrims to pray for the Church, for the pope, for peace, and for himself. And so these petitions became part of our prayers as well. Expressions of gratitude always formed the backbone of our nightly prayers though. We thanked God for all of the blessings of the day. We thanked Mary, Saint Ignatius, Saint James, and the other saints of heaven who companioned us.

Ingratitude, Saint Ignatius believed, is the most abominable of sins "for it is a forgetting of the graces, benefits, and blessings received."[30]

It is our custom to end night prayers with words taken from the concluding blessing of the Divine Office: "Grant us a restful night and a peaceful death."

EIGHT

Don't Worry

Making the pilgrimage was a lifelong dream for Nadia, a young woman from a lakeside village in Switzerland. Nadia started her Camino pilgrimage in Le Puy, France. She had already been walking for two months and had covered close to seven hundred kilometers by the time we started in Saint-Jean-Pied-de-Port. Our pace matched hers, so we often met along the Camino Francés.

Recognizing her thick, long, black hair and bright blue backpack from behind, we would hasten our steps in order to catch up with her. Nadia shared our desire for retreat silence while walking so we did not hike together. Rather we would stop long enough to inquire about each other and find out where overnight lodgings were planned ahead.

It was often a surprise, and always a joy, to encounter Nadia in the various towns and cities of northern Spain. Evie and I would be enjoying our daily ration of green olives at one of the outside tables that line the city plazas, and Nadia would appear from around the corner. We had the pleasure of breaking bread together on several occasions.

In Astorga we enjoyed a traditional, four-course *cocido maragato* meal with Nadia. The hearty supper included a large platter of meats, a bowl of potatoes, cabbage, and beans, and a bowl of thin noodle soup. Savoring this feast gave us plenty of time to talk about our experiences with Ignatian spirituality. I shared with Nadia that I was making the pilgrimage as a way to companion Saint Ignatius. At first, she did not understand who I was talking about since she pronounces his name "Ignaz."

Under the direction of a sister in an apostolic religious community in Switzerland that draws its founding principles from the Society of Jesus, Nadia had recently made the *Spiritual Exercises.* Her spiritual director then encouraged Nadia's desire to undertake the Camino pilgrimage as a way to experience the graces of the retreat "in the world."

The focus of Nadia's retreat was simplicity. It became the theme of her pilgrimage as well. For Nadia, living simply is at the heart of the *First Principle and Foundation,* the opening reflection of the *Spiritual Exercises of Saint Ignatius.*

The *First Principle* is aptly named, not only for its placement and import in the *Spiritual Exercises,* but for what it asserts: first and foremost, we are created to praise, reverence, and serve God. The Camino provided a setting for Nadia to further reflect on this truth and, more importantly, put it into daily practice.

Nadia's insights, and especially her example of living simply, prompted me to reflect on the *First Principle* as well.

How am I praising, reverencing, and serving God in my life?

How have I allowed other things to usurp this "end for which I was created"?

Being materialistic has never been among my legion of vices. Unfortunately, no virtue can be claimed by this trait either. I am simply not attracted to things. Evie notes that absence of virtue whenever I'm sent to shop for a new pair of Levi's and return home without a new pair of Levi's.

"How could that be?" she muses aloud and loudly. "Did the car break down on the way?"

"No."

"Were the stores closed for some special holiday?"

"No."

Similarly, Evie fails to see the good in my lack of acquisitiveness whenever she begins talking about redecorating our condominium.

"Your eyes are glazing over again, Luke."

On my first day of teaching at Jesuit High School in Portland, Oregon, one sophomore interpreted my material austerity positively. I overheard him explain to another student, "Mr. Larson doesn't decorate his classroom because he doesn't want us to be distracted."

That's right, my bright, young scholar.

The number, weight, and functionality of apparel and gear are significant considerations for a five-hundred-mile hike. Camino guidebooks and websites emphasize in particular the importance of proper footwear and a limit of twenty pounds for loaded backpacks. Adhering to these recommendations turned us into reluctant shoppers.

Keeping
Company
with
Saint
Ignatius

104

Evie and I spent most of one day trying on a wide array of lightweight backpacks at a sporting goods store in Minneapolis. I must have fallen victim to what is referred to as "decision paralysis."[31] Faced with a plethora of options, coupled with the desire to make the "right" decision, I found it difficult to choose. As often happens in such situations, the first pack I tried on was the one I ended up purchasing.

I ordered and returned several lightweight hiking boots before finding a pair that fit well. Even then, on several days of the trek, I had to tape parts of my right foot to prevent hot spots from becoming blisters.

Like most Camino pilgrims, Evie and I wore sandals in the evenings and on break days—whenever we were not hiking. We were surprised to see some pilgrims wearing sandals, even flip-flops, as they hiked. Unfortunately, we also saw a number of pilgrims become incapacitated with blisters and other foot problems. Father Tom was one of them. On a doctor's advice, he spent a week in Pamplona to allow his feet to heal before continuing his pilgrimage.

As with my boots, I ordered and returned several T-shirts, shorts, hiking pants, and socks before finding ones that not only fit comfortably, but were also lightweight and quick-drying.

Outerwear consisted of a micro-fleece pullover, a wind-cutting rain jacket, and rain pants. These proved to be a wise choice in staying warm and dry, especially slogging through the torrential rains of Galicia. Silk neckerchiefs—what my cowboy father called "tuf rags," but never scarves—also came in handy, when tied bandit-style around our heads, in keeping black flies out of our noses and mouths.

I enumerate these items simply to note how little we had with us on the pilgrimage. A hanging fish scale indicated our fully loaded packs weighed around sixteen pounds each.

It could easily be assumed that we would be possessive of our few carefully selected articles of clothing and gear. This was not the case. We valued these things only in as much as they were useful. As soon as we realized that something was not necessary, it was left behind.

While we didn't give a second thought to leaving things behind, Camino friends were a different story. That's why we were delighted to come across Nadia again, this time in O'Cebreiro, a mountain village in Galicia known for its round houses with stone walls and peaked thatched roofs called *pallozas*. The humble mountain hamlet is also known for its pre-Romanesque church of Santa María la Real (Royal Saint Mary's), thought to be the oldest church on the French Way pilgrimage route to Santiago. A miraculous holy grail legend goes with it.

Sometime around the fourteenth century, a peasant from another village made his way up the mountain through a whiteout blizzard to the church, compelled by an ardent desire to receive Communion. The priest presiding at Mass thought the poor man a fool for jeopardizing his life and chided him for being out in such abominable weather. He scoffed at his devotion. As he did so, the host on the paten became physical flesh and the wine in the chalice turned into physical blood, the very body and blood of Christ.

*Keeping
Company
with
Saint
Ignatius*

106

According to tradition, the priest repented of his cynicism and, along with the faithful peasant, was later buried in the side chapel where the much-revered paten and chalice are displayed.

We discovered Nadia kneeling before the glass-encased chalice and host. She had been praying there for hours. I marveled at her serenity. She was not anxious about continuing on to Triacastela to find lodging. She was not concerned about lunch. In fact, she was not worried about anything. She was wholly content to be in the presence of Christ in the Blessed Sacrament.

Imbued with Ignatian spirituality, Nadia prays at any time and in any place. She experiences a constant, abiding sense of God's presence. Her relationship with God is like that of an innocent, wide-eyed child, yet it's certainly not immature. It is simple, yet not simplistic or naïve.

Her faith reminds me of one of my favorite movie characters, Tevye, in *Fiddler on the Roof.* Anywhere and at any time, the impecunious milkman raises his arms and voice toward heaven and talks with God like he would his wife, daughters, and fellow villagers. I could imagine Nadia chatting familiarly with God, like Tevye, as she encountered various blessings and hardships walking by herself across much of France and Spain.

Nadia's simple, direct, immediate faith inspired and edified me deeply. It is the kind of faith for which I have long yearned and prayed.

If the opposite of *material* is *spiritual,* then the feeling of not having, holding, or possessing anything material was a spiritual experience. It was liberating to live the Gospel message, at least for a couple months. "So do not worry, saying, 'What shall we eat?' or 'What shall we drink?' or 'What shall we wear?'" (Matt. 6:31)

I didn't worry about my appearance either. In hindsight, I should have adopted Ignatius's early custom of letting his hair "go its way according to nature." Instead I went to the opposite extreme.

Not wanting to spend time and effort finding barbers along the Camino, I shaved my dome about once a week using disposable razors and dabs of nonfoaming cream. More accurately, I would begin to shave when Evie, seeing blood gushing copiously from every hemisphere of my noggin, would yank the "safety" razor from my grip and finish the scalping . . . er, barbering . . . herself.

Afterwards, I would look to Evie for some Band-Aids and a modicum of pity. I received neither. It seems that, in a nurse's way of thinking, gashes and scrapes that do not require a 4" x 4" gauze pad are not worth fussing over.

Writing to Jesuit priests and scholastics (seminarians) in Portugal, Saint Ignatius instructs, "Earthy concerns have no place in your thoughts and affections, you will be preserved from distraction and dissipation, with the result that you will be able to direct your thoughts and affections and employ them in attaining the end for which God created you; that is, His honor and glory, your own salvation, and the help of your neighbor."[32]

While "earthly concerns" may not be my Achilles' heel, there are other things that distract and dissipate my attention away from the end for which God created me.

Trust, for instance, is a persistent, even pesky, theme in my life. It rears its head at more spiritually charged times, such as during retreats and while in the process of making vocational decisions. A poignant example was my anxiety about entering into a marriage that would include a ready-made family of three children, pre-teens at the time.

I feared rejection. I feared hearing words like, "I hate you. You're not my father."

A wise counselor helped me realize that anxiety is the fear of a future that might never come.

In the eighteen years we have been together as a family, the future that I feared so mightily has never come. My step children have given me the precious gift of their love and have never withdrawn it.

Yet trust remains an issue in my life, and so it was no surprise that it tagged along on our pilgrimage. At some point along the Camino, Evie wrote "TRUST-TRUST-TRUST" in the inside cover of her journal. We both experienced the Camino as a laboratory for trusting in God's providence. It is a "wilderness" or "desert" journey of trust, receptivity, and surrender as one leaves behind that which is familiar, secure, and comfortable. It is a time for learning how to let go of the need for control. That is a lesson I pray to "get" so that, on my deathbed, I will be able to peacefully and confidently say, "Into Your hands, oh Lord, I commend my soul."

The Camino guidebooks and websites assured us that there are accommodations at least every nine miles along the route, and most albergues serve an evening meal to pilgrims, so we were not too concerned about food and shelter. Yet there were plenty of other unknowns and variables on the five-hundred-mile trek to put our ability to trust to the test.

Evie's most pervasive fear was that she would not be able to walk the entire way to Santiago. Along with that, she was anxious about the possibility of disappointing me by having to drop out. Frankly, I was worried about that possibility as well. Peeling away even more layers of concern, I feared the possibility of failing to protect Evie from some danger that might arise along the Camino.

The one thing that we could absolutely, positively, unquestionably count on was access to the funds in our bank account. Or so we thought.

Before leaving our home in Fargo, I opened a new checking account with our bank to use for travel expenses in Europe. At the same time, I upgraded our frequent flier credit cards. We received the new debit and credit cards just before our departure but did not receive the separate mailings with our new four-digit PINs.

I didn't think anything about it until we tried to get cash from an ATM in Spain. Our cards worked fine for making purchases but, without knowing our new PINs, we could not get cash. We tried every conceivable possibility, including several calls to our bank and to the credit company. Eventually we learned that we could get cash advances from certain banks using our credit card. But it was far from easy.

Imagine trying to explain our situation to bankers who only understand Spanish. Each time we needed cash we tried at least five banks in the larger cities before a bank official would agree to the cash advance. This was incredibly time-consuming and frustrating. I resented having the peace and solace of our walking retreat disrupted by the pursuit of mammon.

It certainly tested our ability to trust in God's providence. Yet, through the kind assistance of bank officers—with the patience of Job—God did provide.

NINE

Make Haste to Help Me

Like most pilgrims, Evie and I sought lodging in the old section of cities. That placed us close to the cathedrals, central plazas, historic buildings and monuments, and perhaps most importantly, to the Camino. So locating our hotel was simply a matter of finding the cathedral—those enormous structures with the pointy towers.

It was not that easy in León. How could an entire cathedral just disappear? Was magician David Copperfield in town performing one whopper of a magic trick?

A few blocks back we could see the tips of the spires. Now we could not.

"Perdoname."

I caught the attention of an older, well-dressed gentleman nearby.

"¿Donde esta la catedral?"

Apparently I was accenting the wrong syllables because he had no idea what I wanted.

I tried "Iglesia grande."

He began naming the churches in León.

It's a very long list.

"No, no," I interrupted, "Más grande."

At the same time I touched my fingertips together above my head in the shape of a spire or perhaps a miter, the ceremonial head-covering of bishops.

"Ah! Catedral!"

"Si, catedral."

The kind and exceedingly patient man walked with us several blocks until the cathedral was clearly visible ahead. After shaking hands and thanking the gentleman, we laughed heartily as he put his fingertips together above his head while loudly exclaiming, "Mas grande! Mas grande!"

A clerk at the tourism office on the outskirts of Logroño was another person who went out of his way to be helpful, including calling a hotel and making reservations for us. "Muchas gracias" seemed wholly inadequate to express the appreciation we felt. After scrolling through my mental vocabulary list for appropriate words, I intended to say in Spanish, "We are very grateful." Instead I said, "We are very nice."

The gentleman was too polite to even raise an eyebrow at my folly but then joined us in a good laugh as soon as I realized what I had said. As we walked out of the tourism office, Evie observed, "Friendly is friendly in any language."

How true.

At the time Vespers was scheduled to begin in the twelfth-century Church of Santa María, a monk entered the sanctuary and explained that he was the only monk at the small monastery of

San Salvador del Monte Irago in the Galician town of Rabanal del Camino. Other monks from the Saint Ottilien Abbey in Austria would be joining him soon.

My imagination had not been getting as much exercise as my legs so I let it run wild for a moment. I amused myself with the thought of one monk attempting Vespers—choral evening prayer—by himself.

"O God, come to my assistance."

"Excuse me while I run across to the choir stalls on the other side."

"O Lord, make haste to help me."

That did not happen.

Instead the young, ordained monk concelebrated Mass with a priest pilgrim from Ireland.

It was one of the most moving liturgies of the entire pilgrimage. At first the interior of the church, with its achromatic stone, barrel-vaulted ceiling, seemed cold, dark, and cavernous. Then, as the candles were lit and the liturgy began, an almost entrancing worship space was created. During the Prayers of Intercession, pilgrims voiced their concerns for struggling companions and prayed in thanksgiving for all who provided us such gracious and generous hospitality along the Camino. It was truly a Eucharistic, a thanksgiving, celebration.

∽

Whenever possible we lighted votive candles in the churches along the Camino for specific individuals. As a child, lighting a candle for someone usually meant that person was on the "front burner" of my mother's worry priorities. Similarly, Evie and I renewed this devotional practice on the pilgrimage as a way to give tangible expression to our concern for family members, friends, and fellow pilgrims. It was a symbolic way of placing the persons into the hands of Jesus or Mary.

The Cruz de Ferro, or Iron Cross, one of the most emblematic monuments of the Camino, provided another way to express our prayers symbolically, outwardly. Located at the 1,504-meter summit of Mount Irago, the highest point on the pilgrimage route, the metal cross is affixed to the top of a tall oak pole, and at its base is a large mound of pebbles and stones.

Pilgrims traditionally carry with them a small rock from their native land, or at least, like us, from the valley below. These stones are then tossed onto the pile at the foot of the cross. The ritual symbolizes the letting go of sins, guilt, and other burdens that might be rattling around in one's soul.

After adding our stones to the heap, we asked for God's mercy and forgiveness for our sins. We used the opportunity to pray for our family, relatives, friends, as well as our fellow sojourners, past and present, who have humbly placed their petitions before the Lord on this spot since the eleventh century.

Keeping company for Markus, a young pilgrim from southern Spain, meant walking the Camino with Blade, his long-haired, yellow Labrador. We first encountered the pair at a bistro in Ponferrada.

My first impressions of Markus were not charitable. I thought him inconsiderate in allowing his large dog to lie between the

*Keeping
Company
with
Saint
Ignatius*

114

tables, such that servers and patrons had to step over him often. And, as we watched Blade repeatedly lick his sore, bloody paws, I also judged Markus inhumane in conscripting his aged dog on such a grueling peregrination.

"This pilgrimage is difficult for *all* who venture on it," Evie remarked. Empathy comes from a Greek word meaning partiality derived from suffering. I suppose that is why Evie was especially partial toward Blade, a fellow sore-footed creature, as we continued to meet up with him and his master along the Camino.

After talking with Aimeus, a retired businessman from Belgium, I became more sympathetic toward Markus as well.

We were guests at *El Paraiso del Bierzo*, a traditional, rock-walled country inn built at the end of the nineteenth century. The inn, situated just off the road in the farming village of Las Herrerías de Valcarce, overlooks a lush green pasture bordered below by oak and chestnut trees and the clear Valcarce River. A large patio with comfortable deck furniture afforded a perfect spot from which to enjoy the magnificent view while sampling local Mierca wine.

Moments of peace and quiet were punctuated by Aimeus's brief, increasingly frustrating cell phone exchanges from a nearby table. Eventually conceding defeat, he set down his phone and joined us in a raised glass salute to the Camino.

We learned that Aimeus had befriended Markus earlier and had agreed to help him find lodging that would allow Blade inside. This was proving to be an impossible task.

Albergues will admit any dirty, smelly, hairy biped with six euros and a pilgrim's passport. But, if you happen to have four paws and a tail, you are out of luck. This is undoubtedly one of the reasons the Confraternity of Saint James strongly advises pilgrims not to have dogs accompany them on the Camino.

*Keeping
Company
with
Saint
Ignatius*

116

Rural people of northern Spain do not regard dogs as pets, and scoff at anyone who does. In their minds dogs stay outside, ready to protect flocks and farms. Even Aimeus, a man who had made a good living out of persuading others to see things his way, could not convince the locals to take in Markus with his pooch.

Before his conversion, Ignatius spent countless hours day-dreaming about the acts of gallantry he would like to do for an unnamed noble woman. After his conversion, he desired to do great things in the service of Our Lady. Fending off farm dogs in eastern Galicia provided a few chivalric opportunities of my own in the service of my lady.

Spurning its master's commands to return to the farmyard, a massive German shepherd followed us along the cow path, barking and growling at our heels. I turned and raised my walking stick menacingly in the air, which, according to the Confraternity of Saint James, will "only make matters worse." Thankfully, the unruly cur retreated, but not before tipping off its littermate at the farm ahead that lunch is on its way.

The second dog snarled and barked at us from the other side of a hedgerow until we were well past its not-to-be-disputed domain. Believing we were out of danger, I let down my guard. Then the sudden leaping up of hairs on the back of my neck alerted me to impending danger. An image flashed through my mind of the bloodthirsty brute lunging for Evie's throat.

Without turning, I slashed my walking-pole-turned-rapier violently through the air. Ignatius the Soldier would have been so proud of my swordsmanship.

The young pilgrim, who impulsively jerked his bicycle to the side just in time to preserve his skull and its contents, was not so impressed. Suffice it to say that he was not yelling the customary "Bon Camino!" as he wobbled his bike down the stony path trying to distance himself from me as quickly as possible.

While descending along a narrow road into the hamlet of Piero, about four kilometers from our overnight destination of Villafranca del Bierzo, a woman wearing a floral-patterned housecoat gestured vigorously from her backyard for Evie and me to come to her house for something to eat.

She seemed too eager, even desperate, for us to stop, which made us uncomfortable. So we continued on to a neighboring house where red plastic tables and chairs were set up in the open garage and driveway. Although makeshift, this at least bore some semblance to the open-air cafés to which we had become accustomed along the Camino route.

Between sips of our refreshing Cokes, we attempted to string together enough rudimentary Spanish words to convey friendliness toward the kindly proprietor. We began with the universal conversation-starter, the weather. Remarkably, we were able to communicate more than we might have supposed.

Before long we were interrupted by the sight of someone walking slowly up the street toward us. It was the woman who had motioned to us from her yard. She gazed hawkishly at us as she shuffled past, no doubt attempting to confirm her suspicion that her unscrupulous neighbor had once again lured away paying customers with his swanky plastic furniture–filled driveway café. She turned around just past the house and began ambling her way back to her own, her reconnaissance mission complete. Our host mimed his estimation of her sanity by circling his index finger around his temple and pointing toward her back as she trudged dejectedly away.

Keeping
Company
with
Saint
Ignatius

118

With the intravillage rivalry episode over, we continued our chat with the owner of the improvised refreshment stand. A framed black-and-white photograph served as a visual aid in telling us about his wife, children, and grandchildren. We were able to get across that we have children and grandchildren of our own. A second scratched and faded photograph showed our newfound friend as a handsome young man in a military uniform.

Having seen small vineyards on our way into the village, Evie asked if the gentleman made his own wine. In response, he went into his house and brought out an unlabeled bottle of red. He uncorked the bottle and poured two large glasses for us to sample. The homemade wine was made even more delicious by the ardor of our host's cordiality.

Would you like a second glass?

No, no. *Muchas gracias.* We need to be able to walk, not crawl, the remainder of the way to Villafranca del Bierzo.

After overnight stops in Villafranca del Bierzo, Las Herrerías de Valcarce and Triacastela, we chose the 6.5 kilometer longer

Camino route to Sarria in order to visit the Benedictine monastery of San Xulián de Samos. A vista point along the wooded trail gave us our first view of the impressive monastery in the midst of the lush Ouribio River valley.

Continuing the Benedictine's long tradition of hospitality, the Abbey has a ninety-bunk pilgrim hostel in the rear of the monastery. We passed it by, however, and checked in to a quaint, riverside hotel on the edge of Samos. Online reviews claim the hotel is "recommended especially against modern style lovers." I'm guessing that our style of loving is either classical or postmodern because Evie and I did just fine there.

After a late afternoon pasta lunch and siesta, we took a tour of the sixth-century monastery. Floor-to-ceiling murals detailing the life of Saint Benedict along the Gothic and Baroque cloister walls enthralled me the most.

A priest was vested and ready to begin evening liturgy, so the tour had to end abruptly inside the imposing eighteenth-century monastery church. We stayed for Mass and Vespers, the great prayer of the evening in which the end of the day is so beautifully and solemnly consecrated to God.

Afterwards the resident monks joined us in the pews to listen to performers in period costumes sing about the medieval Camino de Santiago. Music was used to promote important pilgrimages, such as Saint James' Way, in Spain and throughout Europe in the Middle Ages. It was an integral part of the pilgrimage experience itself. It offered a way for pilgrims who spoke different languages to communicate. And the songs, often devoted to the Virgin

Mary, helped fortify pilgrims for the arduous journey to their destinations and home again.

The music we enjoyed that evening at San Xulián de Samos originally came from medieval manuscripts such as the *Codex Calixtinus* and *Llibre Vermell*. The musicians used reproductions of instruments depicted in manuscripts and on church portals of the Middle Ages. The devotional songs and hymns enchanted us. The processionals and Spanish folk melodies made us want to get up, parade around, and dance right along with the performers. Such songs had a similar effect in the Middle Ages. The *Llibre Vermell*, or Red Book, of fourteenth-century music from the monastery of Montserrat instructed pilgrims on how to behave:

> As it happens that the pilgrims, while holding night vigil in the church of the Blessed Virgin of Montserrat, sometimes desire to sing and to dance and even so during the day, in the church square, where only virtuous and pious songs may be sung, some suitable songs have been written down here for this need. These should be used in a respectful and moderate manner, so as not to disturb those who wish to continue their prayers and religious contemplations.

Did Ignatius desire to sing and dance, perhaps in jubilant celebration of his conversion, on the mountaintop of Montserrat?

After laying his sword at her feet, did Ignatius honor the Black Madonna with a Basque folk dance, elegant and solemn, during his night vigil?

It's a splendid image.

TEN

A Banquet Is Prepared

S ome pilgrims walk or peddle their way to Santiago over much greater distances and longer periods of time than we did. For instance, there was that couple whose bicycle pilgrimage began at the doorstep of their home in Belgium.

Others make the pilgrimage incrementally over the course of several years. And still others are satisfied to travel only part of the Camino route. Many in this last group start in Sarria in order to travel the requisite 100 kilometers to the Cathedral in Santiago, which qualifies them for the Compostela, the official certificate of completion.

I respect completely each of these approaches to the Camino. I understand the constraints of time and resources. And I feel inestimably blessed to have been given a sabbatical leave and grant funds that made possible both the leisure and means necessary to walk the Camino from Saint-Jean-Pied-de-Port to Santiago in one trip.

You might think that, filled with profound gratitude, there wouldn't be much room left for judging others. Yet, to my shame, I did.

Perhaps God, in his infinite mercy, will cut me some slack for keeping my critical thoughts mostly to myself.

I resented the loud, daypack-toting "privileged pilgrims" the most. After spending all morning working up an appetite for half an apple, Snickers, and a gulp of warm water, we would come across one of these groups occupying every picnic table at a shady, roadside rest area. A sumptuous feast of sliced meats, local cheeses, fresh fruits, breads, and salads would be spread before them, complete with bottles of wine and iced water.

Stacked inside nearby vans would be large duffle bags stuffed with changes of clothing and personal items. After lunch these would be delivered to a hotel, along with any of the group who had grown weary strolling along on a full stomach. Hopefully fatigue and hunger reduce culpability for such judgmental thoughts, especially since, as noted above, I really do believe that there are many legitimate ways to accomplish "the Way."

I think of the Camino as a metaphor for the kingdom of God, similar to the parable of the workers in the vineyard found in the Gospel of Matthew (Matt. 20:1–16). All are welcome to share in the Eucharistic banquet of the Pilgrims' Mass in the Cathedral of Santiago, regardless of whether you have walked five hundred miles or five miles to get there. In the same way, all of the laborers in Jesus's parable receive the same wage, one denarius, regardless of the hour of the day in which they began working.

Of course, it is no surprise that those who arrived earlier and did more work would envy those who did less, yet received the same pay. Likewise, it is natural for pilgrims who have walked from Saint-Jean-Pied-de-Port to feel that they have "earned" their Compostela more than those who began in Sarria. Yet, just as the vineyard owner tells the grumbling workers that he has a right to do whatever he wishes with his money, Jesus reminds us that all is gift, all is grace. The doors of the Santiago Cathedral swing wide for all without regard to merit. So, too, are the gates of the kingdom opened by God's love and mercy, which cannot be earned.

As Evie and I marched along the Camino in the mornings, with the sun rising in the east behind us, our elongated shadows seemed indistinguishable from those that might have been cast by a pilgrim couple five hundred years ago. It brought such a couple to my imagination frequently.

What must it have been like to make this pilgrimage during the Middle Ages?

Records from that era give the impression that early Santiago pilgrims were mostly from the lower strata of society. With little money, they had to settle for the rather austere, communal lodgings of hospices and monasteries. In those with beds, rules usually limited the number of pilgrims per bed to two. In those without beds or cots, strangers huddled together on straw mattresses on the floor "warming each other with the compound body heat of their tired limbs."[33] Rosemary, lavender, chamomile, and other sweet-smelling herbs were strewn around them to mask the smells.

Not all pilgrims were indigent, however. Some carried hefty titles, both civic and ecclesial, to and from Santiago, albeit on horseback or in carriages, accompanied by large retinues of attendants. There were also numerous pilgrims who belonged to the class of prosperous merchants and artisans. These had the means to ensure a hot meal, a jug of wine, and a bed of their own.

Then, as now, pilgrims are simply people. Nobility or peasantry, rich or poor, French or Spanish, our longings, hopes, fears, and dreams are pretty much the same. And so are our shadows.

It is a misnomer to think that the hardships endured by medieval pilgrims must somehow be approximated in order for modern pilgrimages to be authentic. Pilgrims in the Middle Ages didn't say to themselves, "I'm going to huddle between other stinky pilgrims under a mangy blanket on a pile of old straw on a cold, plank floor as an example for future generations of authentic misery." No, unless early pilgrims were looking for penitential opportunities, they sought the best lodgings and provisions they could afford.

Each person has to determine for themselves what is authentic on pilgrimage and in life. For us it meant walking everywhere we went for the entire forty eight days from Saint-Jean-Pied-de-Port to Santiago, including side trips. Staying in hostels, rural houses, and hotels as often as possible didn't detract from the authenticity of our experience. As it was, my hide was bitten twice by bedbugs early on our journey. That was plenty of that particular brand of misery.

Our Camino pilgrimage was truly Ignatian, not only for the places we visited but for the principles and practices of Ignatian spirituality we embraced along the way. For instance, I employed both the daily Examination of Conscience and the Discernment of Spirits in attempting to resolve a conflict toward the end of our pilgrimage.

I will describe the Examination of Conscience, or the *Examen*, more fully in a later chapter. Suffice it to say that the *Examen* is a way of recalling and reflecting on God's presence within the events of the day. The Discernment of Spirits offers its practitioners a way to put those reflections into action.

Discernment, as explained in Ignatius's *Spiritual Exercises*, helps us align our desires with what God desires—both in what is desired and in the way that it is desired. It helps us orient ourselves away from pride and selfishness and toward our deeper, more authentic desires.

Evie had entrusted much of the details of our trip to me. And so I planned that, after spending two days in Santiago, we would continue on foot to Finisterre, concluding our walking pilgrimage on the Atlantic coast. That plan was put into jeopardy by Evie's aggrieved feet and her struggle just to keep going while still a week away from Santiago.

Evie wanted to feel that she had truly done the Camino with our arrival at the Cathedral of Santiago de Compostela, the traditional destination of the Way of Saint James. She wanted to be proud of her accomplishment, certainly not to feel that she had failed because she was unable to walk another four or five days beyond Santiago.

On the other hand, I wanted to be able to count myself among the handful of pilgrims that hike on to *Finis Terra*, to the end of the earth, as it was considered in medieval times.

I wanted to stick to our plan. OK, *my* plan.

I wondered why, after a couple days of rest in Santiago, Evie didn't think that she could keep going. After all, she had made it this far.

*Keeping
Company
with
Saint
Ignatius*

126

I suggested that she take a bus to Finisterre, check into a nice hotel, and pamper herself while waiting for me to arrive on foot. This was my magnanimous compromise, with *pampering* thrown in to sweeten the deal. Yet, in my heart of hearts, I knew that it would never work.

At first my pride and selfishness resisted the attitude of indifference that is an essential prerequisite for Ignatian discernment. Indifference is the neutral or balance point between the teeter-totter of inclinations. It suspends the choosing of one alternative over another until it is determined which one is more for the glory of God.

I was anything but indifferent. I wanted to continue on to Finisterre. I wanted, not God's glory, but my own.

The irony of claiming an Ignatian pilgrimage while stubbornly blocking the possibility of discerning God's will eventually illumined my conscience. After a few raps on my noggin from Ignatius's celestial walking stick, I began to realize that keeping company with Evie was my first, and more authentic, desire. This thought left me with what the Saint called spiritual consolation. In contrast, thoughts of separating from my wife in Santiago left my spirit in turmoil, in desolation.

While making our way to Santiago through a torrential downpour, I told Evie that I no longer wished to continue on to the coast. And so, as we paused atop the *Monte del Gozo*, the Mount of Joy—where, if it had been a clear day, we would have been able to see the cathedral spires of Santiago for the first time—we embraced each other with joyful, peaceful spirits.

In his Camino guidebook, John Brierley suggests an air of detachment in entering Santiago: "That way you will not set yourself up for euphoria nor for disappointment."[34] Nevertheless, we experienced a sense of letdown as we approached the cathedral. Evie later wrote, "It could not compare to the emotions of walking with Jesus, Mary, Luke, Nadia, and so many others toward a destination that is not the real 'destination.' Santiago is not *the* destination."

After rounding the enormous cathedral on our way to the Hotel de los Reyes Católicos, we spotted Markus and Blade among the crowd of arriving pilgrims. We congratulated Markus with a handshake and Blade with a scratch behind his floppy ears. In spite of inordinate challenges, they had made it.

We assumed Marcus had found accommodations for both himself and Blade somewhere in Santiago. But we didn't ask.

The Hotel de los Reyes Católicos, otherwise known as the Parador Santiago de Compostela, shares a corner of the sweeping *la Plaza del Obradoiro* (in Gallego, *Plaza do Obradoiro*) with the cathedral. It was originally built in 1499 by the Spanish monarchs Ferdinand and Isabel as a huge, cross-shaped hospital to shelter and care for poor and sick pilgrims. During those first days of November, the historic hotel sheltered not only us but numerous Vatican officials, along with media people from around the world.

They were there preparing for the apostolic visit of the pope in observance of the *Año Santo Jacobeo* or Jacobean holy year, which occurs whenever the feast day of Saint James, the 25th of

July, falls on a Sunday. We watched the construction of an enormous white stage on which the Holy Father would celebrate an open-air Mass in *la Plaza del Obradoiro* just three days after our departure from Santiago.

Pope Benedict XVI expressed his high regard for holy pilgrimages during his Compostela Holy Year address: "I express my special closeness to the pilgrims who have come and who will continue to come to Santiago. I ask them to treasure the evocative experiences of faith, charity and brotherhood that they meet with on their journey, to experience the Way especially inwardly, letting themselves be challenged by the call that the Lord makes to each one of them. Thus they will be able to say joyfully and firmly at the Portico of Glory: 'I believe.'"[35]

Wearing hiking clothes, we were conspicuously underdressed at the Parador, especially with so many well-heeled dignitaries all around us. Yet that didn't stop us from exploring the four magnificent cloisters of the hotel and dining on fish and meat dishes cooked *a la gallega* in the luxurious dining room.

After a restful night in the hotel, we readied ourselves for the Pilgrims' Mass in the cathedral, considered by many to be the culmination of the Camino de Santiago de Compostela. It was All Saints' Day, which provided a fitting opportunity to celebrate and appreciate Saint Ignatius, Saint James, and other holy men and women of heaven who had been keeping us company on the Way to Santiago.

As Evie observed that morning, I was "high with excitement," which is a nice way of saying that I was chattering like a caffeinated chipmunk. Evie claims, with some justification, that words come out of my mouth before my eyes open in the morning.

My mother, bless her soul, had tried to warn Evie before we were married. She claimed that God would hold me accountable for my idle words—something about lots of time in purgatory. No doubt she was influenced by Saint Benedict's esteem for silence. He quotes Proverbs 10:19 in his Rule governing monastic life: "In a flood of words you will not avoid sin."

Ignatius would agree. In his notes about the *General Examen* he wrote, "One should not speak 'idle words,' by which I understand those of no profit to either myself or to others, and those not directed to that end."[36] He also considered ill-directed or aimless talk a sin.

My ace in the hole was making the pilgrimage during a Holy Year. I was about to attend Mass, go to confession, pray for the intentions of the Holy Father, and give a donation to the cathedral. In fulfilling these conditions in Santiago, I would bag a plenary indulgence, a full pardon from all that time in purgatory. So, as I was saying. . . .

Since it was All Saints' Day, we knew the Santiago Cathedral would overflow with people at the noon Pilgrims' Mass. We arrived about 10:30 a.m. in order to secure seating.

We not only found spots in a front pew but, more significantly, we found Nadia, our friend and fellow pilgrim from Switzerland. Nadia had attended an earlier Mass and was planning to stay for the Noon Liturgy as well.

While settling in next to each other for the long wait, Nadia whispered that she had something to show us after Mass. What could it be? Her saucer eyes, beatific smile, and birthday girl excitement indicated it must be something quite special.

As soon as the archbishop followed in the long procession past us at the conclusion of Mass, Nadia led us through the throngs of people, past the chapels of San Andres and San Antonio, to the chapel of Santa Catalina. "See! See! It is Our Lady of Lourdes!" Nadia beamed.

Before us was a statue of Mary standing in a shallow grotto with Saint Bernadette Soubirious kneeling at her feet. The scene depicts the appearances of the Blessed Mother to Bernadette, a peasant girl from Lourdes, in 1858.

Nadia had told us about her special devotion to Our Lady of Lourdes during one of our earlier conversations. Like us, Nadia was grateful for the companionship of Mary on the Camino. Discovering the shrine in one of the side chapels of the Santiago Cathedral was a tremendous surprise gift for Nadia, one she was eager to share with us, her new friends.

We later received a card from Nadia telling us that, after finishing her walking pilgrimage at Finisterre, she visited the Shrine of Our Lady of Lourdes in southern France to again thank Mary for keeping her company during her solitary trek across much of France and Spain.

∽

Many miracle healings and other interventions have been attributed to Saint James over the centuries. Some of the books about the Camino tell of experiences along the Way that, while perhaps not miraculous, were still perceived as having divine influence.

*Keeping
Company
with
Saint
Ignatius*

130

About halfway through our pilgrimage, I developed an ear infection, which steadily worsened until my right ear was completely blocked. I couldn't hear anything out of it. So I began to desire a miracle of my own.

I called upon Saint James—not the apostle, not the pilgrim, not the Matamoros (killer of Moors), but the thaumaturgis—the miracle worker. I also called upon Saint Ignatius, Saint Luke, and the Blessed Mary. Yet my prayers for instant, miraculous healing seemed to fall on deaf ears among my heavenly intercessors. God, I supposed, was waiting for just the right, dramatic moment within the legendary Cathedral of Santiago.

Perhaps, after climbing the narrow, well-worn steps behind the main altar and reverently laying my hands on the shoulders of the massive statue of Saint James, my ear would be suddenly and miraculously unstopped. It didn't happen.

Perhaps as the high-swinging Botafumeiro, a gigantic silver censer, filled the enormous eleventh- to twelfth-century edifice with incense before the Pilgrims' Liturgy, a beam of light would shine down from one of the stained-glass windows above the altar, and my ear would be instantly cured. It didn't happen.

Plan C was to find a doctor.

Tuesday morning, the day before we were scheduled to depart, Evie and I walked several kilometers through the narrow streets of Santiago's historic quarter to a medical clinic. Fortunately, the receptionist spoke English and so I was better able to explain my need. She offered to make an appointment for me to see an ear, nose, and throat doctor later that week. Dejected, since that would be too late, we turned to leave. Then she added, "Unless you can come back at 5:30."

"That would be perfect!"

That evening, using an awkward blend of Spanish and English, I told the ENT doctor about the problems with my ear. She removed the blockage and then asked if I could hear again. I could think of only one response.

"Es un milagro!"

I had gotten my miracle in Santiago.

As we stood to follow the crowd of pilgrims out of the Santiago Cathedral in the evening of All Souls' Day, I felt a desire for the Sacrament of Reconciliation. It seemed like a fitting way to conclude my spiritual and sacramental pilgrimage.

I waited by one of the many confessionals that line the nave. When it was my turn, I approached the booth, open in the front, and inquired, "English?" The priest shook his head and pointed toward another confessional. At one confessional after another I repeated, "English?"

"No, Español solomente."

"Spanish or Italian."

I became frustrated because I believed that, given a chance, I could have found a way to communicate both my sins and my contriteness to any one of the confessors. My sins are rather boilerplate after all. None involve rumpled sheets, a cash register, or an ax. Pride could be pantomimed easily enough with a few Tarzan chest thumps and a self-satisfied grin. I'm not sure what I might have done to indicate lust but, with the improvisational skills learned in Mrs. French's high school speech class, I was sure that I could come up with something.

After I had run the gambit of confessionals, and as the lights of the cathedral were being turned off for the night, a priest took pity and agreed to hear my confession.

I was handed a two-page, laminated menu of sins in English and instructed to point to the ones I had committed. Simple enough, except that I had trouble finding any that matched my particular brand of wretchedness.

No, I have never taken home a stapler from my place of employment. No, I do not use the name of God to express anger or surprise.

So I resorted to pantomiming. I stuck my nose in the air haughtily and thumped my chest a couple times with my fists.

The priest must have had a steaming plate of *pulpo a feira* (fresh octopus) and a nice bottle of Ribeiro waiting somewhere, because he hurriedly absolved me of all my sins and then quickstepped out a side door of the cathedral.

ELEVEN

At Home with Ignatius

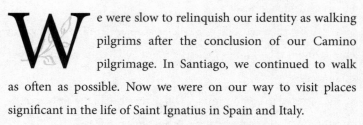

We were slow to relinquish our identity as walking pilgrims after the conclusion of our Camino pilgrimage. In Santiago, we continued to walk as often as possible. Now we were on our way to visit places significant in the life of Saint Ignatius in Spain and Italy.

Forensic anthropologists tell us that we leave physical traces of ourselves wherever we go. They count on this trace evidence to solve crimes. Given that human beings consist of both a body and a spirit, I wonder if we leave, not only physical traces of ourselves, but spiritual ones as well. Might spiritual "traces" of Ignatius remain in Azpeitia, Manresa, and Rome?

Call it what you will, I believe that a certain holiness lingers in these places and others, touched by the holy man from Loyola. The events in his life occurred, not only at a particular time of history, but at specific places. I read and reread about these events in the *Autobiography of Saint Ignatius* (which I certainly recommend).[37] Now I was eager to actually visit the places where these events of Ignatius's life took place. Trekking across the Basque lands of

Íñigo's heritage, and crisscrossing the paths of his many journeys, served to kindle my desire to experience these places firsthand. I wanted to linger for a time in holy spaces.

Getting to these places required trains, buses, and taxis, all of which sped through the countryside much, much too rapidly. I was melancholy as our train from Santiago sped eastward past some of the towns through which we had recently walked. I was already missing the slower pace, the picturesque villages, and the people—mostly the people. Yet the long train ride back across northern Spain confirmed that we had completed a substantial journey by foot.

The apron strings of a doting, grandmotherly Basque ensnared us at the bus station in the coastal city of San Sebastián on the Bay of Biscay, about twenty kilometers from the French border. After pointing to seats she expected us to occupy on the bus, she made sure that the driver knew to let us off at the Shrine of Loyola in the Basque country of Gipuzkoa, Spain.

It was my desire to keep company with Saint Ignatius that had provided the impetus for our Camino pilgrimage. It was Ignatius who came to mind most often as we passed through the villages, nestled beneath green, sheep-speckled hillsides of his Basque homeland. Now, at last, here we were in Azpeitia, where Íñigo Oñaz López de Loyola was born in 1491, the youngest of thirteen children. Having accepted an invitation to visit, I felt like I had arrived at the home of a dear friend.

"Welcome," Ignatius might have said. "Make yourselves at home."

Keeping
Company
with
Saint
Ignatius

136

From the bus stop we walked toward the imposing dome of the Mudejár-style Basilica. We decided to go first to the Tower House, the ancestral home of the Loyola and Oñaz family. The hosts at the front desk epitomized hospitality befitting the "Holy House." They invited us to visit the Basilica while they set up the audio narration system in English for us.

A question posed by the *Santuario de Loyola* website spoke to my dichotomous feelings as we entered the Basilica. Were we there as curious visitors, tourists, or pilgrims? "In a certain sense," the website ruminates, "it does not really matter, because as you visit the home of one of the men who greatly influenced history and the milieu in which he changed the course of his life, the pilgrim hidden in you may surface."[38]

I was immediately awestruck by the grandeur of the Basilica's interior, with its continuous circular nave interconnected to the central space by eight trumpet-shaped arches. My reaction took me by surprise, perhaps because I had felt more "at home" in the simple, village churches than in the grand, ornate cathedrals of the Camino.

Our attention was drawn first to the central niche of the Spanish Baroque main altar. There, surrounded by resplendent inlaid marbles, is a silver statue of Saint Ignatius modeled after one that we would later see in the Church of the Gesù in Rome. From the main altar, we slowly made our way around to the side altars. As we paused at each of the statues, I felt like I was introducing Evie to close friends.

I was.

"This is Francis Xavier, one of the first companions of Saint Ignatius and renowned for his missionary work. It is his family castle we are going to visit tomorrow."

"Here is Francis Borgia from the famous—or infamous—Borgia family. After his wife died, Francis relinquished his title as Duke of Gandía to his eldest son to become a Jesuit priest."

"Here is Alphonsus Rodríguez, a lay brother Jesuit known for his piety."

"This is Peter Claver. He's best known for his devoted ministry to African slaves in Columbia. It is believed that he died, like your mother, of Parkinson's."

Evie needed no introduction to Mary, of course. We took a moment to thank her once again for keeping company with us on our pilgrimage.

Here I am not claiming that Mary and the Jesuit saints are actually present within the statues. Although in her book, *Mary, Mother and Warrior: The Virgin in Spain and the Americas*, Linda B. Hall notes that, for some believers, Mary's presence is experienced "in the representation, not apart from it."[39]

My claim is simply that Mary, Ignatius, and others are truly present to me—are actually keeping company with me—in the communion of the saints. Images of them are reminders of that abiding presence. I agree, then, with Hall's conclusion: "The Virgin, as a human and accessible person *re-presented* in an image, becomes a conduit between the human being and the divine."[40]

After circling the interior of the Basilica twice, and spending time in prayer, we were ready to explore the Tower House of

Loyola. From its northeastern outside corner, the two distinct parts of the large house are readily apparent. The lower half, with its two-meters-thick stone walls, looks like a castle fortress. The upper brick half, with its numerous windows, looks more like a red brick house.

Eagerness and excitement elbowed past each other on their way into the Holy House. I would have rushed right up to the third floor, the location of Ignatius's conversion, had it not been for the audio narration that directed us from one point of interest to the next—and from one floor to the next—of the fortified home.

Aquí Se Entrego á Dios Iñigo de Loyola.

These words, painted on the center ceiling beam in Ignatius's bedroom, told me that I had finally arrived.

Here Ignatius of Loyola surrendered to God.

A vision of the Blessed Virgin Mary with her Son in her arms was a key event in the conversion of Saint Ignatius. The scene is magnificently depicted by a statue in the Chapel of the Conversion—what had been Ignatius's third-floor bedroom. The statue shows Saint Ignatius seated on a bench with an open book in his left hand, presumably either the *Life of Christ* or *The Lives of the Saints*, and his right hand outstretched in a gesture of receptivity to the blessed vision before him. The carved, polychrome sculpture captures incredibly well the enraptured radiance of the Saint at that moment.

That appearance was just the first of many Saint Ignatius had of Our Lady. Although some were more distinct than others, all increased his devotion to her, such that he gave serious thought to killing someone he believed had insulted the Blessed Virgin while on his way to Montserrat.

Were we detached, observational tourists? No.

There, in the Holy House, I internalized the truth that it is the journey within that makes you a pilgrim.

෧

Standing at the bus stop later that afternoon, Evie and I began to wonder if we were going to have to be *walking* pilgrims again. Several bus drivers wagged a finger at us indicating their bus is not one that would take us back to San Sebastian.

Our bus finally came, relieving us of the growing feeling of rejection. We arrived in San Sebastian just in time to catch another bus to Pamplona, where we stayed overnight.

The next evening we went by bus to Javier, the birthplace of Saint Francis Xavier, patron saint of Navarre and the missionary church.

We spent time in the attached basilica the next morning while waiting for the rest of Xavier Castle to be opened to visitors. There I experienced a special closeness and devotion, not to Saint Francis Xavier as might be supposed, but to Mary, the mother of God. Undoubtedly it was the softly illuminated statue of Mary above the main altar that drew my attention. The figure of Mary, with hand gently outstretched, evokes a sense of warmth and tenderness beyond what might seem possible in a statue.

The image helped me envision the apparitions of the Blessed Virgin Mary at Lourdes. In response to questions or requests that were either imprudent or naïve, Saint Bernadette claimed that

Mary simply smiled or laughed. What a beautiful image—Mary, the mother of God, smiling and laughing as she keeps company with us on our pilgrimage through this world!

Keeping
Company
with
Saint
Ignatius

140

Evie and I were the first visitors that mist-shrouded morning, and so we walked through the castle by ourselves—quietly, peacefully, reverently. Listening to the audio narration in Francis's room in the Tower of Homage, I was fascinated to learn how accomplished Francis Xavier was in his studies, sports, and social pursuits at the Collège Sainte-Barbe in Paris.

It was there that Francis Xavier first befriended Peter Favre and later Ignatius Loyola. Together with James Lainez, Simon Rodríquez, Alfonso Salmerón, and Nicholás Bobadilla, these men pronounced private vows in a small chapel at Montmartre on the Feast of the Annunciation in March 1534, thus becoming the First Companions of what was to be the Society of Jesus.

I enjoyed seeing the various paintings and sculptures of San Francisco de Javier in the castle museum. I appreciated the dioramas that depicted the significant events of Saint Francis's life, beginning with his birth in the family castle in 1506 and ending with his death on an island on the southern coast of China in 1552. Yet, of all of the things in the castle, I was most affected by the thirteenth-century Crucifix of the Smiling Christ, carved out of walnut, in the Chapel of the Holy Christ.

Jesus appears peaceful, serene, with a parted-lip smile on his face as he hangs on the cross. This unusual image has elicited many questions, and as many speculations, over the centuries. How is it possible to represent Christ as smiling from the cross? What is the sculptor trying to suggest? What is the theological rationale for this portrayal of Christ?

Such were not my questions. I was not curious. I was simply moved by the image of Jesus smiling.

What a powerful image it is: Jesus, in horrific agony, smiling down at us. At that moment, it was personal.

Jesus was grinning at me, as if to affirm that he had accompanied me every step of the way to Santiago. He walked with me. I walked with him, in the company of the saints from Loyola and Xavier.

Ignatius's pilgrimage in 1522 took him first to Montserrat, where he hung his sword and dagger at the foot of the Black Madonna, and then on to Manresa, where the future saint spent almost a year praying, fasting, tending the sick, and recovering from his own bouts of illness. There he was referred to as the "sack man" because of the simple, threadbare cloak that he wore. They also called him the "holy man" because of his continual praying, penances, and the virtuous life he led. More importantly for us, it was in Manresa that Ignatius had the mystical experiences that inspired him to write the *Spiritual Exercises*.

Travel considerations necessitated that Evie and I visit these places in reverse order, Manresa before Montserrat. We stayed at the Jesuit Spirituality Centre in Manresa, where from our window we could see the Cardoner River below, the imposing Gothic Basilica of the Seu to the right, and the high, jagged crags of Montserrat ahead in the distance.

As overnight guests we had after-hour access to the Holy Cave, *la Santa Cueva*, where we prayed in quiet solitude as Saint

*Keeping
Company
with
Saint
Ignatius*

142

Ignatius had done five hundred years ago. Access for us meant descending an interior stairwell of the Spirituality Centre. For Ignatius, it meant making his way up the rocky hill through thick brambles and underbrush to the cave.

The *Avantcova*, or Cave's Hall, is the ornately decorated ante-chamber of the cavern. It was the space of worship until the eighteenth century, when the church was constructed adjacent to it. The lavish iconography, stained-glass windows, mosaics, bronze medallions, and other architectural and artistic features are all intended to prepare visitors to enter the most sacred part of the building, the cave itself.

Above the altar in the back of the cave is an alabaster relief showing Saint Ignatius writing the *Spiritual Exercises*, inspired by Jesus and Mary, in the shelter of the shallow cave or grotto. Transfixed on the image, I prayed.

Here in your cave, Saint Ignatius, I feel like I have arrived. I feel at home. You instruct your spiritual followers to use their senses and their imaginations in prayer. I'm imagining the dampness, the coolness, and the dimness of this humble cave when it was as you found it. I picture you here in your rough-cloth tunic and sandals. I imagine your countenance radiant in the presence of Jesus and Mary. I imagine you jotting the notes that would become your Spiritual Exercises. I'm amused to envision you taking breaks from your writing to chisel these two crosses in the side wall of the cave. It makes it all seem more real somehow.

Thank you for companioning us on our pilgrimage, Saint Ignatius. Thank you for modeling for us what it means to be a pilgrim. I wanted our sabbatical pilgrimage to be a time of walking with Jesus in your company. I was not disappointed. Now that I have experienced what it is like to walk with the Lord as you did, simply for the sake of keeping company, I desire more. Continue to walk with us, Saint Ignatius, as we follow in your footsteps around Manresa . . . and in all of life. Amen.

༄

The next morning, the friendly, helpful clerks at the Manresa Office of Tourism supplied us with a map of other places to see along the "Trail of Saint Ignatius" in Manresa. The first point of interest was one of the most prominent monuments in Manresa, the Old Bridge, *El Pont Vell*.

Medieval bridges fascinate me for their beauty, their construction, and their age-old continuity. They were among my favorite sights along the Camino. Yet this one, dating to the Romanesque period of the fifteenth century, held particular interest because it was crossed so often by Ignatius, it was just below his cave, and it was in its shadow that Ignatius had some of his most profound mystical experiences along the banks of the Cardoner River.

After crossing the high-arched bridge, we became lost trying to find the Sanctuary of Our Lady of Guidance, the first place Ignatius might have visited upon arriving in Manresa and where he had a vision that led him to the cave. In Ignatius's day, the rocky road between Montserrat and Manresa passed right by the chapel. It was customary for pilgrims and other wayfarers to commend themselves to Our Lady in the Sanctuary before leaving Manresa and to pray in gratitude for her protection there upon their return.

Keeping
Company
with
Saint
Ignatius

144

One of the young tourism clerks walked us to the site of the Hospital of Saint Lucía, which was destroyed during the Spanish Civil War. Once inside, she showed us to the Rapte Chapel of the Abduction, the place where Ignatius's soul was taken into heaven while he was virtually comatose for eight days.

Ignatius spent most of his time in Manresa at the hospital, attending tirelessly to the poor and the sick. The austere living conditions and servile work helped complete Ignatius's transformation from soldier to saint. This experience eventually led to what are called *hospital experiments*, in which Jesuit novices spend several weeks caring for the sick and dying in hospitals, hospices, and nursing homes. The "experiment" is meant to educe humility and prime fledgling Jesuits for the ministerial life of the Society.

My own Jesuit hospital experiment took place at what was then Saint Helen's Hospital in Chehalis, Washington, a small town midway between Portland and Seattle on Interstate 5. I slept across the street in a mostly empty house owned by the hospital and joked that "the hardest thing about my hospital experiment was the broken spring in the middle of my mattress." Every waking hour was spent at the hospital providing spiritual care, Eucharistic ministry, and assisting the nurses on the medical/surgical floor and in the emergency department.

Routine work was accented by watching surgeries and accompanying the medics on transports. I loved every minute of it. The experience confirmed my call to pastoral ministry, which led to my early career as a certified hospital chaplain. The seeds of my healthcare ministry were thus planted, five hundred years before my birth, at Saint Lucía Hospital in Manresa.

An arrow at the edge of the route map indicated that the Santa Maria de la Salut's Sanctuary at Viladordis, our one remaining site to visit, was some distance from the others.

After walking quite a ways, Evie and I stopped a young woman on the sidewalk to inquire about the location of the church. Using a combination of Spanish and hand gestures, Miriam explained that it would take an hour to walk but only a few minutes by car. We accepted her gracious offer of a ride. On the way we picked up her son Aleix at his school. His elementary school English was sufficient to aid in translating while we became acquainted.

Miriam and Aleix waited at their car while Evie and I went inside the small Romanesque church where Saint Ignatius spent entire nights on his knees before the Virgin Mary and her Son, Jesus, and where he was graced with many heavenly visions. We knelt for only a couple minutes at the iron grating, not wanting to keep our gracious friends waiting. Yet it didn't take long to absorb the holiness of the chapel, built in the tenth century.

The blessing of seeing that holy place was magnified inestimably by the kindness and generosity of Miriam and Aleix, who have taken to heart the biblical imperative to be hospitable to strangers in their midst.

As Ana María Pineda points out in her essay on hospitality, the Greek word *xenos*, meaning both "stranger" and "guest," signals the essential mutuality that is at the heart of hospitality. "No one is strange except in relation to someone else; we make one another guests and hosts by how we treat one another."[41] Miriam and Aleix turned us from strangers to instant friends by the kind and gracious way they treated us.

Saint Ignatius visited the Chapel of Our Lady of Viladordis frequently. Neither Miriam nor her automobile were around to transport him. Instead he used the 2.5-mile walk as a way of keeping company with Jesus and Mary. We can be assured of this because of the roadside crosses and sanctuaries he prayed at, and the visions he received, along the route. It is completely implausible that Ignatius would spend entire nights on his knees in the church then shut off his prayer, like water from a faucet, while walking to and from Viladordis.

We had already gained an understanding of the vast distances Saint Ignatius covered on his pilgrim journeys. Yet retracing the Pilgrim's footsteps around Manresa helped us to appreciate how often he walked shorter distances, mini-pilgrimages if you will, as a way of companioning Jesus and Mary.

Ignatius's mini-pilgrimages are instructive for those of us who desire our own. First, he left his cave. Likewise, it is good for us from time to time to step away from all that is comfortable—and confining—in our caves. This includes our large screen television, laptop, tablet, e-reader, and, yes, even our smart phone. Second, Ignatius had an intention, a purpose. Ours might be to seek guidance, forgiveness, healing, love, or simply the opportunity to walk in the company of Jesus for a few blocks. And third, Ignatius had a destination. Ours might be a local church, shrine, grotto, convent, monastery, or other place marked by God's fingerprints. The place is not as important as the ability to check out of the "too busy" of our lives and to recharge our spiritual batteries while there—and while on the way.

After tromping around the vicinity for eleven months, the adopted son of Manresa bid farewell to his friends and followers, saying, "So long as I am alive you will remain in my hearts and when I reach heaven I will pray for you."[42] Taking that blessing into our own hearts, we continued on our way.

ᔈ

From Manresa we took a train to the foot of Montserrat Mountain and then rode the Cremallera Funicular, the rack and pinion railway, up its precipitous cliffs to the famous Benedictine monastery.

Arriving at Montserrat on March 24, 1522, Ignatius changed into pilgrim's attire, hung his sword and dagger at the foot of the altar of Our Lady, and then kept vigil before her through the night.

High above the altar of the Basilica is the Black Madonna, *La Moreneta* in Catalan, a wooden statue of Mary seated with the Child Jesus on her lap. The sculpture represents Mary as the mother of God in Majesty and the Throne of Wisdom. She holds the sphere of the universe in her right hand. And with her left she offers us the Child Jesus, the fruit of her womb. Jesus blesses us and holds a pineapple, symbol of life and fruitfulness.

Dating from the twelfth century, the origins of the statue are uncertain. I'm going with the story that it was carved by Saint

*Keeping
Company
with
Saint
Ignatius*

148

Luke in Jerusalem before making its way to Spain, where it was lost before its discovery by shepherds on Montserrat.

After descending from the Madonna chamber, I paused to light a candle and place it among hundreds of others that softly illumine the outside wall of the Path of Ave Maria.

Mary, mother of Jesus, I remember my mother lighting votive candles like these. And, as a child, I remember her saying "offer it up" in response to complaints about life's aches and pains. Now I offer up the bedbug bites, weariness, hungers, blisters, and other hardships of our pilgrimage for whatever spiritual benefit they might gain our loved ones.

I reflected momentarily on Ignatius of Loyola in this holy place. Here he "offered up" the misery of his injured leg. More importantly, he offered up his status as a soldier of nobility and became a humble pilgrim. What is more, he became a companion of Jesus.

Thank you, Mary, for placing us with your Son on the Camino. Thank you for accompanying us every step of the way from the Porte Notre Dame of Saint Jean to the Cathedral of Santiago. Please remain with us, watch over us, as we rest and retreat here at Montserrat. Amen.

Then I stopped to pray in one of the lateral chapels of the Basilica dedicated to Saint Ignatius. And I paused once again to pray at a statue of Saint Ignatius in a recessed portico before exiting the atrium.

Before the throngs of tourists arrive in the morning and after they depart in the late afternoon, the monastery is a gloriously quiet, peaceful setting for repose and retreat. These times of sunrise and sunset, framed by the abbey and mountain crags, were breathtakingly spectacular.

I savored Lauds in the early mornings, Mass at midmorning, and Vespers in the early evenings in the Basilica at the Abbey of Santa María de Montserrat, followed by hymns sung by students of the world famous L'Escolania choir school. My mind could not understand the words chanted in Catalan, the official language of Catalonia, yet the psalms and prayers of the monks transcended linguistic barriers to fill my soul with their sacredness and beauty.

⌐

Evie and I had planned to be at Montserrat two nights but stayed a third because we weren't ready to leave our high mountain retreat.

From there we took trains to Barcelona where we had reservations at a hotel near the Gothic Quarter. We had shipped a box of clothes to the hotel before traveling to Europe so that we would have nicer attire to wear in the hotel, and especially in the fine dining room. The four-star accommodations were to be a way of treating ourselves to a bit of luxury after the hardships of the Camino.

As pilgrims we had carried only bare essentials yet, like Saint Paul, in "having nothing" we felt that we were "possessing everything" (2 Cor. 6:10). Now, surrounded by ample possessions, we found ourselves dispirited. We were struggling to relinquish our pilgrim identity. We weren't ready to return to the "real world." We weren't ready to be Frommer's Portable Guide–toting tourists.[43]

The next day we walked fifteen blocks to the Church of the Holy Family (*La Sagrada Família*) designed by the modernist Catalan

*Keeping
Company
with
Saint
Ignatius*

150

architect Antoni Gaudí. It is said that one either loves or hates Gaudi's work. Peering up at the church's façade while waiting in a long line to enter, our opinion teetered toward the latter. The exterior looks like towers of melting ice cream with fruit topping. Our opinion softened as soon as we were inside though.

My attention was drawn first to the modern stained-glass windows, through which a kaleidoscope of brilliant colors stream into the nave. I moved to the center and turned around slowly as my eyes followed the massive supporting columns to the tree-like canopy of the ceiling. Despite being unfinished, the church's interior is truly awe inspiring.

Next, Evie and I walked about three kilometers to the Barcelona Cathedral (*La Seu*) in the center of the Gothic Quarter of Barcelona. By this point, Evie had reached—exceeded, actually—her church touring limit so she sat in a pew while I walked around to the twenty-eight side chapels and through the fourteenth-century cloister with its small chapels, gardens, fountains, and a gaggle of thirteen white geese. I paused to pray at the Xavier Chapel.

I've heard about how you hobbled around Japan, Francis Xavier, with blistered and swollen feet. So I thank you all the more for your empathic companionship on the Camino, especially as Evie struggled to keep walking with her own painful feet. Thank you for modeling what it means to be both called and sent forth for the sake of the magis, the more, the greater honor and glory of God. You truly were a man for others in this life. You remain so now from your place among the communion of saints. Stay with us as we travel on to Rome to spend more time in the company of your dearest friend, Ignatius. Amen.

We had visited Loyola, Montserrat, and Manresa—a few of the more significant locations in the life of Ignatius. However, a journey with the intention of following in the Saint's footsteps would not be complete without also visiting the places in Rome where he spent seventeen years as the leader of the newly founded Society of Jesus.

An overnight train transported us to the Eternal City, whereas Ignatius made the journey on foot, along with two of his companions, in 1537. The three stopped to pray at a roadside chapel in the village of La Storta, just outside of Rome. There Ignatius had a mystical vision of God the Father placing him with his Son, which confirmed his desire to remain always— along with his companions—in the company of Jesus. Ignatius also heard God say to him, "I will be propitious to you in Rome."

Propitious is not a word you hear every day. Perhaps that is one of the reasons this translation of the divine pronouncement is so memorable. Yet it is the assuredness of the declaration that stands out for me. God made it definitively known to Ignatius that he would be favorable to him and his companions in their future together in the company of his Son, Jesus Christ.

At the urging of Pope Paul III, Ignatius and his companions remained in Rome, teaching, preaching, caring for those in poverty, and giving the *Spiritual Exercises*. Through the course of those early ministries, Ignatius recognized that God intended for him to remain in Rome, and eventually to establish the Order's head-quarters there. In his lifetime, the Society of Jesus grew from eight to more than a thousand members, with houses and colleges all over Europe and as far away as Ethiopia, Brazil, and Japan. Indeed, God fulfilled his promise to grace Ignatius in Rome, and well beyond.

My prayer while in the Holy City was to be favored with an experiential sense of Ignatius's life in his later years as superior general of the Society of Jesus. Our tours included Ancient Rome, the Catacombs, the Vatican, and we were fortunate to attend a General Papal Audience. Yet what I desired to see most were the rooms of Ignatius on the top floor of the Piazza del Gesù. As soon as the doors were opened to the public for the day, I scurried through the hallways and up the stairs.

A Jesuit from Croatia warmly welcomed us and offered to guide us through the residence. He began by explaining that four rooms are all that remain of the original house. Here in this compact apartment—a combination bedroom and study area—Ignatius lived simply and prayed fervently, often with tears of joy streaming down his cheeks. Here, on a little desk, he wrote and revised the Constitutions of the Society of Jesus, along with more than seven thousand letters. Here he received dignitaries and governed the worldwide Jesuit Order. And here he died on the morning of July 31, 1556.

A few articles on display helped me to better visualize the saint who had been keeping company with us for the previous two months. In the office area is a bronze head made from the original death mask of Ignatius. The bronze is on a pedestal showing his rather short physical stature. Ignatius's vest, cloak, and chasuble helped me image him as well. Yet it was his tattered shoes that evoked a sense of who he was the most. I contemplated all of the journeys, long and short, he had taken while wearing them. For Saint Ignatius, every journey was a pilgrimage. He saw his entire life as a pilgrimage, a journey with Jesus and to Jesus. A feeling of spiritual profundity washed over me as I reflected on, of all things, a pair of simple leather shoes.

The next day we visited the *Chiesa del Gesù* (Church of the Holy Name of Jesus), the mother church of the Society of Jesus. There I knelt and prayed before the imposing and lavishly decorated tomb of Saint Ignatius. My prayer was mostly a litany of thanks to Jesus for his companionship, and that of his friend, Ignatius of Loyola.

Thank you, Jesus, for walking with us across northern Spain. I am grateful for your sending Saint Ignatius to keep us company as well.

Thank you for my Ignatian spirituality. Thank you for the chance to share it more profoundly with Evie these past couple of months on pilgrimage.

Thank you for Joan, Louise, Sister Pilar, Father Tom, Father Steve, Greg, Nadia, John, Simon, Chris, Miriam, Aleix, and all of the holy women and men, of both heaven and earth, who befriended and companioned us along the Way of Saint James and afterwards.

Thank you for my desire to be more attentive to you and to those you bring into my life. Thank you for the sense of hungering for your nearness. Thank you for the experiment in trusting that was the Camino. And thank you for all of the consolations, and even the desolations, along the Way.

Thank you, Lord Jesus, for being so propitious to me and my family. Amen.

TWELVE

Hearts Burning Within

Like many couples, Evie and I have "our song." It is "The Rose," made famous by Bette Midler in 1979. Violinists played it in the background while I proposed to Evie, and a cantor sang it during our wedding Mass. The lyrics "some say love, it is a hunger, an endless aching need" are especially indicative of my spiritual life.

Most often I experience my relationship with God as a *hunger*—an endless aching longing, yearning, desire. This hungering is not a sense of emptiness or absence though. Rather it is like what I experience when I'm especially close to Evie, physically, emotionally, spiritually. In my love's embrace, my desire for her intensifies. Similarly, that sense of hunger is most intense at the times when I feel closest to God. Such was the case on the Camino. I experienced the Way as a place of abiding presence—God keeping company—yet also as a place of longing.

"Our hearts are restless until they rest in Thee, O Lord." Saint Augustine had it right.

A sense of my sinfulness, my unworthiness, often accompanies that hunger, which brings to mind Simon Peter's first encounter with Jesus. Recognition of being in the presence of holiness caused Peter to immediately fall at Jesus's feet saying, "Go away from me, Lord. I am a sinful man!" (Lk. 5:8).

Like Peter, I often cannot imagine Jesus wanting to keep company with me, a sinner.

Give me a chance to rinse off the fishy smell of my sins first. Then we can hang out.

But Jesus does not go away. Instead he draws nearer. "Then Jesus said to Simon, 'Don't be afraid; from now on you will fish for people.'" (Lk. 5:10).

It was Jesus's idea for us to make the Camino pilgrimage so that we could spend time with him. It was his invitation, his plan. Jesus was with us, not like a divine babysitter out of obligation or necessity, but because he wanted to be.

Out of his own experience, Saint Ignatius believed that Jesus is always eager, even excited, to be with us and to give himself to us without reserve, much more than we are to receive him.

"It is characteristic of Him to wish to give us greater graces than we are ready to receive, and to dispose us to desire and hope from His divine liberality that He will fulfill and even surpass our hopes and desires."[44] Jesus generously and lovingly anticipates us, says Ignatius, and continues to offer himself to us, even when we rebel against him.

The Gospels are replete with images of Jesus Christ walking along and talking with those whom he wanted to be with. In the course of his ministry, Jesus walked a great deal throughout the region of Galilee. It was along the Sea of Galilee where Jesus invited Simon Peter and the other fishermen to join him, to walk with him. They immediately left their boats and did just that.

*Keeping
Company
with
Saint
Ignatius*

156

These walks were eventful, to say the least. Multitudes cried out and reached out as Jesus and his disciples passed by. Some brought their children. Some climbed sycamore trees. All wanted something, expected something, of Jesus. They sought inner peace, healing, forgiveness, inspiration, enlightenment, or simply to be in the presence of holiness.

Yet not everyone who watched and waited for Jesus to come up the road had good intentions. Some were there to find fault, to trip him up. Nothing ruins a nice walk on a sunny Sabbath afternoon than to have a bunch of nit-picking Pharisees accuse you of harvesting and threshing—of working—simply because you had plucked a few heads of grain to munch on while strolling through a wheat field.

Of course, there were also the uncommitted disciples and would-be disciples, such as the rich young man who, instead of walking with Jesus, walked away from him. They were fine with hanging around the man from Nazareth as long as he stuck to feeding the crowds and healing the sick. But then Jesus began referring to himself as the Bread of Life, from heaven no less, and spelled out to them the cost of true discipleship. This was too much. And so they turned and walked away.

Walking was quality time for Jesus. It was a way to be alone with, and to keep company with, the disciples who stuck around and continued to be his followers. These walks engendered some incredibly weighty conversations. For instance, on the way to Caesarea Philippi, Jesus questioned his disciples, "Who do people say that I am?" After a few off-target guesses from others, Peter responded, "You are the Christ."

Even in his resurrection appearances Jesus chose to walk with others. One story begins, long before Coast Guard boating regulations, with seven men crowding onto a small boat. They didn't catch any fish while out all night on the Sea of Galilee. Little wonder, since they were doing more brooding over the death of Jesus than actual fishing.

At daybreak the risen Jesus invited them to a hearty breakfast on the beach. While the disciples were finishing the last morsels of charcoal-grilled fish and bread, Jesus said to Simon Peter, "Let's take a walk along the shore." Thus Jesus took Peter aside to take care of some unfinished business.

As they strolled along the sand, Peter professed his unequivocal love for Jesus three times. Jesus then restored Peter to full discipleship and commissioned him to shepherd his flock, the church.

In another story we hear of two disciples walking along the dusty road to Emmaus lamenting the horrific crucifixion and death of Jesus the Nazarene, whom they had hoped would be the Messiah. Jesus joined them and asked what they were discussing. They answered by summarizing the events of the previous few days. Then, beginning with Moses and the prophets, Jesus interpreted for them the Scriptures that pertained to him.

Later that evening, after recognizing Jesus in the breaking of bread, they said to each other, "Were not our hearts burning within us while he talked with us on the road and opened the Scriptures to us?" (Lk. 24:32).

⏝

Ignatian spirituality is centered squarely in Jesus Christ. It is, therefore, preeminently incarnational, that is "in the flesh" from the Latin *incarnare*. God became a man, Jesus of Nazareth, so that he could walk with us, talk with us, and otherwise relate to us in "enfleshed" ways. That remains as true today as it was for the people of Galilee over two thousand years ago.

Ignatius's incarnational spirituality is grounded in the belief that God is present and active in all aspects of everyday life—work, play, studies, art, music, sports, nature, and so on. Everything can be a source for prayer, for keeping company with God. So, for Ignatius, prayer was not about withdrawing from such activities. Instead, he called his followers to be "contemplatives-in-action," reflective people who remain active in the world and who see God in all things. Moments of contemplation can occur right in the midst of our activities.

Contemplation in action also means that we bring our entire selves, our whole beings, to prayer. Sometimes referred to as the *marketplace saint* and the *saint of this world*, Ignatius invites us to enter into the Gospel mysteries with our eyes, ears, noses, taste buds, fingers, and, yes, our feet. Ignatius invites us to "practice the seeking of God's presence in all things," in our conversations, our walks, in all that we see, taste, hear, understand, in all of our actions, "since His Divine Majesty is truly in all things by His presence, power and essence."[45]

All of what God gives us is meant to speak to us. God always desires to keep company with us: to share his love, care, and concern for us. Lovers want to put their love in action more than in words.

This book began, not with the account of a sabbatical pilgrimage in 2010, but a few eons earlier in the Garden of Eden. I began there to show that, from the moment of our creation, God has desired to keep company with us.

That is the very reason we were created. Yet, in drawing us back to the story of our creation, I left out the part about Adam and Eve becoming rather snooty, to the point of thinking they could be gods unto themselves.

That's when we began to throw apples at each other. And what is worse, we went from wanting to keep company with our Creator to wanting to keep our distance. We began to perceive God, not as an intimate companion, but as a harsh judge with a humungous naughty-or-nice ledger.

Yet God never changed. Only our perception of God has. We continue to be the apple of God's eye. We don't have to try to convince God to be with us. God chose to keep company with us long ago.

William Barry, SJ, puts it this way: "One could read the Bible as a testament of God's dogged determination to convince us of the seriousness of *his* desire for a relationship of intimacy with us as a people and as individuals."[46]

That determination culminates in God becoming human and dwelling with us. And, just as God invited us in the beginning, Jesus invites us now, "Get up and walk!"

THIRTEEN

Here and Now

ew people know how to take a walk," claimed Ralph Waldo Emerson. "The qualifications are endurance, plain clothes, old shoes, an eye for nature, good humor, vast curiosity, good speech, good silence and nothing too much."[47]

I like the qualification about plain clothes and old shoes. It speaks to the sense of ease, comfort, familiarity, and informality we most often associate with taking a walk. Yet it is the last qualification that I like the most. There is "nothing too much" we need to know, say, or do in order to take a walk. Granted, if your household includes small children, *every* activity takes a certain amount of effort and patience. However, for the most part, taking a walk doesn't require much forethought or planning. Walks often happen "on the spur of the moment."

If you are taking a walk with the sole purpose of keeping company with someone, then "nothing too much" is really all you need to be concerned about. That's the beauty of leisurely strolls. And that's the beauty of *keeping company*. There are no goals, no objectives, and no outcome measures to achieve. There is no technique to learn, practice, and get right. There is no project to complete. It's *being with*. And it's really that simple—like a walk in the park.

Although simple, keeping company is—by no means—a passive activity. Merely sitting next to a stranger, like one might in a movie theater, is not keeping company. Rather, it is exemplified by the parent rocking a sick child back to sleep at 3:00 in the morning. Or the person who is keeping vigil at the bedside of a dying loved one. Keeping company calls for attentiveness, attunement, involvement, connection. It often entails active listening. Yet even in silence, the bond is no less strong.

We must stand before we can walk. And standing, in itself, is a stance of readiness, attentiveness. Then, as we put one foot in front of the other, we have movement. We move from readiness to action. This movement is always toward or away from something or someone. It is relational.

Walking increases a sense of connectedness. First, you are walking for the purpose of keeping company with Jesus. Second, you are relating to yourself through quiet reflection. Third, you are greeting, if not visiting with, others whom God has placed along your path. And, fourth, you are relating to the world outside of your home or workplace—even if you are a mall walker and that world includes Bloomingdale's, Old Navy, and Foot Locker.

The kind of walking I am suggesting incorporates all of these dimensions. It is a stance of attentiveness to whatever God, and perhaps God through others, wants to share with you. It is holistic action—involving our bodies, minds, and spirits—for the sake of relationship.

Early in our relationships, especially our romantic relationships, we cannot wait to be with each other, to spend time together. Then the demands of life and work pile up and keeping company with the ones we care most about often falls by the wayside. Yet shared activity is the catalyst for strengthening relationships, deepening intimacy.

So be there for each other. Be there *with* each other.

Watching TV or surfing the Internet isn't going to cut it. Instead, dig that old pair of sneakers out of the closet and take a shoulder-to-shoulder walk together.

When taking a stroll with your spouse or a good friend, are you preoccupied with yourself?

"Am I walking the right pace?"

"Am I saying the right words?"

"Am I wearing the right clothes?"

More likely, while walking or hiking with someone you care about, you aren't focused on yourself at all. You aren't judging what you are saying or not saying. You aren't thinking about your appearance. Instead, the focus of your attention is on your walking companion and on the surroundings you are enjoying together.

The reason walks are so relaxing and enjoyable is precisely because they are so unselfconscious. The conversations are usually free-flowing—one minute serious, the next filled with light-hearted banter and laughter. The periods of silence are comfortable. The pacing is natural.

As children, my siblings and I plagued our parents with an endless stream of "what if" questions.

"What if dogs could fly?"

"What if milk wasn't white?"

Thankfully, I have long since given up that pesky habit of asking such seemingly unanswerable questions. Yet it seems appropriate to sneak one in here.

What if, like Evie and me, Jesus invited you to take a walk with him? How would you respond? Would you lay down the nets of your time, your schedule, your plans, and follow Jesus out the front door?

We must always approach the divine with reverence, an attitude of profound respect. After all, we're talking about being in the presence of Jesus Christ our Lord, the one who, at the mere mention of his name, "every knee should bow, in heaven and on earth and under the earth, and every tongue acknowledge that Jesus Christ is Lord, to the glory of God the Father" (Phil. 2:10–11). However, being reverent doesn't mean that we must always be on our knees with our backs straight and our hands folded. Jesus calls us, not servants, but friends (John 15:15). As such, he invites us to relax and be ourselves in his company, to walk with him like we would with a spouse or best friend.

Practically speaking, that means starting your walk with some kind of acknowledgement of Christ's presence, just as you would begin any encounter or activity with anyone. As you head out the door, say something like, "Thank you for inviting me to take a walk with you this morning, Jesus."

This is important, not for making Christ present, but for becoming conscious of his presence.

164

And then you simply walk.

Self-conscious thoughts and pious preconceptions about what you ought to say and do divert your attention away from simply being with, keeping company with, Jesus.

"Is my pace slow and deliberate enough for 'prayerful walking'?"

"Am I aware of my breathing?"

"Does this count as 'prayer'?"

"If I stop to talk with Mr. Hofmeister, would that be a 'distraction'?"

Shake such thoughts from your mind, like pebbles from your shoes, and get back to simply enjoying the walk.

Whenever I take a walk with someone with whom I am comfortable, we sometimes go blocks, even miles, without talking. There is nothing that needs to be said. However, there may be times when you want to talk with Jesus while on your walks together.

If you would like some help getting started, or would like some structure to your conversation, Saint Ignatius offers the Examination of Conscience, or simply the *Examen.* It is a form of prayer that can easily fit into one's regimen of daily walks. The *Examen* is recommended for the morning, midday, and evening, which coincides well with the times of day most of us take our walks.

After reverently acknowledging and thanking Jesus for his presence, I begin a mental scan of my day. I recall getting up early to prepare oatmeal for Evie while she readied herself for work. I recall an office e-mail congratulating me on the successful completion of a project.

Saint Ignatius instructs us to recollect our desires, feelings, moods, attitudes, and inclinations as well. For instance, I felt loving and rather munificent while stirring oatmeal at 5:00 a.m. And Mark's e-mail message left me feeling valued and affirmed.

With increased faithfulness to the *Examen*, during the pilgrimage and since, I have become more routinely aware of such blessings—whether occurrences or feelings, whether large or small, whether pleasant or unpleasant. This increased awareness is, in itself, a blessing. I am continuously awed, and humbled, by how involved the Holy Spirit is in my life.

Incidentally, *Paraclete*, the word Jesus used for the Holy Spirit, means "one called alongside." It evokes the image of someone walking beside another as a protector and guide. Recognizing this divine presence, while recounting the graces of the day, naturally leads to appreciation. I stay with that feeling of gratitude for a few blocks. I find myself spontaneously repeating, "Thank you, Lord."

As my walk progresses, I call to mind the instances during the day when I failed to recognize or turned away from the graces offered me. For example, I might recall how gruff I was with the clerk at the convenience store this morning and consider how my actions might have impacted her day. Or I might recall my participation in a disparaging conversation about a coworker at lunch. Then I ask the Lord to forgive my sinful actions and omissions, and to help me to be more aware of how my variable moods and attitudes affect my interactions with others in the future.

The *Examen* is not naval-gazing. Yet a Y-chromosomal examination of my moods reveals a direct connection with my belly. Just ask Evie. She sometimes carried energy bars in the outside pocket of her pack on the pilgrimage, not because she feared becoming stranded without food. Rather, she feared becoming stranded without food *with me*.

Finally, as I'm rounding the corner back to our condo, I think about the rest of the day, or the day ahead, and I pray to not only know God's will but to fulfill it through the help of the Holy Spirit.

As Ignatius instructs, I conclude such a walk with a colloquy, a relaxed conversation, as I would talk with any dear friend. Mostly my colloquies are simply expressions of gratitude, "Thank you for walking with me, Holy Spirit" or "Thank you for spending this time with me, Jesus."

For Saint Ignatius it was essential that the daily *Examen* begin and end in prayer. It is the difference between a mere stroll and what Ignatius refers to as a "prayer period."

Some workplaces allow three breaks a day, including a bit longer one for lunch. With or without incorporating the *Examen*, these are good opportunities for one-mile sabbaticals. Or you might prefer to walk before or after work, in the mornings and evenings, when you have time to more fully relax in the company of Jesus.

This book promotes walking as a way of simply and routinely keeping company with Jesus Christ and with others you invite along. Walking is only the means, however, and only one means at that. I'm certainly not suggesting it as an alternative to church attendance. You might consider walking to church, as Evie and I did on the pilgrimage and continue to do back in Fargo. This gives us time to prime our prayers.

Nor am I suggesting prayerful walking as an alternative to community service. Walk to the food bank, hospital, or homeless shelter for your next volunteer shift. And, by all means, walk down the street to visit Myrtle, the homebound widow you've been meaning to see for a while. Be sure to ask her what it was like to walk five miles to school in waist-high snow as a child.

↬

Evie and I realize the enormity of the blessing we received in having the time and financial ability to travel to Spain and walk for forty-eight days along the Camino pilgrimage route to Santiago. We also realize that not everyone has such time and means. Yet if our experience has piqued your interest in making a pilgrimage, please don't discount the possibility out of hand. Put it near the top of your bucket list, well ahead of climbing Kilimanjaro.

The Camino can be accomplished quite reasonably, especially when undertaken in the off-peak seasons of spring or fall. Staying in albergues and ordering from pilgrim menus minimizes expenses.

Many pilgrims make the Camino in increments of one or two weeks over the course of several years. Others choose to complete only the last one hundred kilometers of the Camino on foot, or the last two hundred kilometers if cycling, both of which qualify them for an official certificate of completion.

An enticing alternative to the Camino de Santiago is the *Camino Ignaciano*—the Ignatian Way. It is a new walking and cycling trail that retraces the route Saint Ignatius walked from Loyola to Montserrat and Manresa in 1522. A small group of Jesuits and their lay collaborators have mapped out the four-hundred-mile route and have marked it with orange way-finding arrows. They have also divided the route into twenty-seven daily walking segments, and cataloged accommodations and services along the way. The *Camino Ignaciano* website includes daily reflections, based on the *Spiritual Exercises*, for pilgrims to use on the journey.[48]

Early trekkers of the *Ignatian Way* report experiencing a sense of the Saint's presence, seemingly sharing with him the natural and historical wonders of his Basque homeland.

There are as many reasons for undertaking a pilgrimage as there are pilgrims. Some want to grow in their faith or respond to a crisis of faith. Some seek physical or spiritual healing. Some go to do penance. For me, the pilgrimage was simply a way of keeping company with Jesus and others, of both heaven and earth, guided by the example of the Holy Pilgrim from Loyola.

The last entry in Evie's pilgrimage journal reads simply, "I did the Camino to be with You."

Anticipating his pilgrimage to the Holy Land in the Jubilee Year of 2000, Pope John Paul II spoke of the benefits of faith-inspired journeys: "To go in a spirit of prayer from one place to another, from one city to another, in an area marked especially by God's intervention, helps us not only to live our life as a journey but also gives us a vivid sense of God who has gone before us, who himself set out on man's path, who does not look down on us from on high, but who has become our traveling companion."[49]

If the history-steeped Camino de Santiago de Compostela or Ignatian Way are out of the question, there are pilgrimages closer to home. Actually, any sacred place can serve as a pilgrimage destination. A day trip to a nearby basilica, cathedral, or shrine may serve well for someone who is unable to travel farther. As with any spiritual exercise, it is the intent of the pilgrim that matters, not the destination.

Whether undertaking a pilgrimage to a celebrated shrine such as Santiago de Compostela or just circling the neighborhood, you might consider inviting one or two from among the legion of saints, our friends in high places, to keep you company.

Treat yourself to some time with Saint Ignatius of Loyola. Walking across his Basque homeland of northern Spain, Evie and I gained an appreciation for the vast distances and rugged terrain he traversed in life. He certainly believed in walking as a spiritual practice and will empathize with any whose physical limitations make it an ascetical practice as well. Whether you're trying to figure out what to do next in life or if you just want to companion Jesus, you can count on Ignatius's prayerful presence all along the way.

Saint Francis of Assisi is another saint who spent much of his life on the go, even making a pilgrimage to Santiago around 1214. Saint Bridget of Sweden and her daughter Saint Catherine would also be wonderful walking companions. After traveling to Rome in 1348, they spent the next quarter of a century making pilgrimages, including one to Jerusalem.

You might have another holy woman or man in mind, such as a patron saint, to invite along on your peregrinations across town or, perhaps, across northern Spain. In rambling around with the saints, we get, not only models of sanctity, but also glimpses of how passionately Jesus desires to keep company with us all.

Early in this book, I mentioned how much I have missed the annual eight-day retreats that were such a significant part of my life

Keeping
Company
with
Saint
Ignatius

170

as a young Jesuit. Those retreats centered around four or five prayer periods each day. After a moment of quiet reverence, I began these times of prayer by asking for the grace I wished to receive. Then I would spend about an hour meditating on Scripture passages or contemplating scenes in the life of Christ. I would then conclude the prayer period with what Saint Ignatius called a "colloquy," a friendly conversation with Jesus.

These hours of more formal prayer had, as you can see, distinct beginnings and endings. However, the retreats did not start and stop with the prayer periods. In between, I attended Mass, wrote in my journal, did some spiritual reading, exercised, ate, brushed my teeth, and slept. During the eight days, it was all "retreat." It all counted.

Similarly, from the first step to the last, the Camino was a retreat, a pilgrimage. The sore-footed walking, the Coke breaks, the hand-washing of clothes, the conversations around outdoor plastic tables, the liturgies, the late-evening pilgrim meals were all part of the retreat, all part of the pilgrimage.

I tried to convey a sense of this by simply recounting the events, reflections, and insights of the Camino—from trust issues to fending off farm dogs—without any distinction between what was spiritual and what was not, what was retreat and what was not, what was keeping company and what was not.

It was all spiritual, within the context of a holy pilgrimage and sabbatical. It was all retreat. It was all keeping company—with Evie, Jesus, Mary, Saint Ignatius Loyola, Saint James the Greater, other pilgrims, locals, and with me.

The morning and early afternoon hours spent walking along the Camino were somewhat like the prayer periods of my Jesuit retreats. I say "somewhat" because they were not as focused or structured. Nevertheless, Ignatian spiritual practices, such as asking for the grace I desired, imaging events in the life of Christ, and colloquies with Jesus, ebbed and flowed rather effortlessly as I trekked along the footpaths of the Camino. I cherished these times of quiet prayer and reflection, and was rather protective of them.

Gradually I loosened the grip of control on these "prayer periods"—and eventually on the pilgrimage itself—as I realized that my one and only desire was to be with Jesus and others, including Evie and Saint Ignatius. In doing so, I stepped off the treadmill of self-effort, became less self-conscious, and simply enjoyed the company of Jesus Christ and others.

Walking, I came to see, was the one activity that reliably gave me time, apart from the business as usual, to truly keep company with our loving and compassionate God and with others whom God has brought into my life. I realized that it is possible to quiet down without slowing down, at least completely. The desire to share this simple—yet no less profound—insight was the impetus for this book.

It's enough just to be with God, to walk with God, as our earliest ancestors did in the Garden and as we all hope to do in the new and everlasting Eden of heaven.

"Life is all about *practicing for heaven*," notes Richard Rohr. "We practice by choosing union freely—ahead of time—and now.

Heaven is the state of union both here and later. *As now, so will it be then.* No one is in heaven unless he or she wants to be, and all are in heaven as soon as they live in union."[50]

Yet even as we anticipate everlasting life with God in heaven, Dietrich Bonhoeffer admonishes us to remain fully present in the here and now: "I believe that we ought so to love and trust God in our *lives*, and in all the good things that he sends us, that when the time comes (but not before!) we may go to him with love, trust, and joy. But, to put it plainly, for a man in his wife's arms to be hankering after the other world is, in mild terms, a piece of bad taste, and not God's will."[51]

It's enough, and more than enough, to let God be God and to simply be his people—here and now.

Like thousands of other pilgrims, I discovered that, when we walk humbly with our God, we do not have to search for grace. The thin places open up, the veil lifts, and grace abounds. For Ignatius, being a pilgrim means abandoning ourselves into God's hands and allowing ourselves to be formed by that grace.

Evie and I didn't walk the Camino Francés pilgrimage route to earn God's favor, to gain spiritual insights, to obtain remittance for our sins, or to accumulate blessings. We simply wanted to companion Jesus, just as Saint Ignatius did over five hundred years ago and as his followers continue to do today.

This book chronicles the numerous ways in which I strayed from that humble purpose. It records my many failures at attentive listening, at attunement, at intimacy, because of my pride, selfishness, stubbornness, and a host of other sins. It pulls back the curtain on my mixed motives, competing desires, and judgmental thoughts. Yet this misses the point.

This book is not about my stumbles, my feeble attempts at keeping company. Rather it is about giving God praise and thanks for keeping company with Evie and me, on the Way of Saint James, and on our pilgrimage through life. And, even when my sins cause me to be like Cain, a wandering sojourner in the land east of Eden, at the end of my days I pray to hear God say, as he did to King David, "I have been with you wherever you have gone" (2 Sam. 7:9).

Saint Ignatius encourages his followers to "never lose sight of the fact that we are pilgrims until we reach [our heavenly country], and we must not let our affections tarry in the hostelries and the lands through which we pass, lest we forget our destination and lose our love of the last end."[52]

Let us tarry no longer, then, in returning to that question, that personal invitation, posed at the beginning of this book:

Would you like to take a walk?

Acknowledgments

Many people gave me support and encouragement—and terrific quotes—in the writing of this book. Jon Sweeney and the staff at Paraclete Press contributed to its editing, design, and publication. Chris Lowney took time away from his own writing projects to pen its magnificent foreword. Thank you.

Rye, Lacy, Callie, Andrew, and Tim cheered on our pilgrimage from their homes in Montana. Thank you. And thank you for our adorable grandchildren.

Patricia Cahill, Esq., Sister Peggy Martin, OP, Sister Barbara Hagedorn, SC, Tom Kopfensteiner, STD, Jeffrey Drop, along with the National Mission Group, the Fargo Office of Catholic Health Initiatives, and the mission leaders of the Fargo Division, made possible my sabbatical leave and pilgrimage. Thank you.

Marcia Collyer, Mandy Corliss, and Ann Weiss coached me through times of self-doubt and discouragement in the writing of this book. Thank you.

Joan Pollard, Louise Boisvert, Father Steve Linehan, Father Tom Hall, CSP, Greg Tehven, Nadiejda Kirianoff, the Religious of the Sacred Heart of Jesus, Miriam Massana, and Aleix Rafael Massana befriended and companioned us along the Way of Saint James and afterwards. Thank you.

Father J. K. Adams, SJ, offered us his Masses and prayers. Tom and Leslie Sams also kept us in their prayers during our trek across northern Spain. Thank you. I beg pardon and peace of any who are keeping company with me in this pilgrimage of life and whose names I have failed to mention. Thank you all.

Chronology of the Life of Saint Ignatius of Loyola

1491   Birth of Íñigo Oñaz López de Loyola in Azpeita in the Basque province of Guipuzcoa in northern Spain. The youngest of thirteen children.

1506–16 Page in the household of Juan Velázquez de Cuéllar, treasurer of King Ferdinand of Castile, in Arévalo near Valladolid.

1517   Service with Antonio Manrique de Lara, Duke of Nájera and Viceroy of Navarre.

1521   Right leg shattered and left leg wounded by cannonball during the French siege of Pamplona. Operations, convalescence, and conversion.

1522   Montserrat visit. Eleven-month stay in Manresa. Holy Cave, Hospital of Saint Lucia, vision at River Cardoner.

1523   Pilgrimage to Jerusalem.

1524   Studies Latin in Barcelona.

1526   Studies arts and philosophy at University of Alcala. Arrest and trial by Inquisition.

1527   University of Salamanca. Second and third trials.

1528   Studies humanities and theology at the University of Paris.

1534   Pronounced vows along with First Companions at Montmartre.

1535   Theology studies in Venice.

1537   Ordained priest. Move to Rome. La Storta vision.

1538   First Companions regroup in Rome. After one year's wait, proposed move to Jerusalem seen to be impossible; meets strong opposition in Rome, overcome by recourse to pope; acquittal at trial.

1539   Deliberations about new Society of Jesus.

Keeping
Company
with
Saint
Ignatius

176

1540	Society of Jesus founded by papal bull from Pope Paul III.
1541	Preliminary draft of Constitutions. Election as superior general. First solemn profession of vows. Departure of Francis Xavier to India.
1542–43	Work with prostitutes, Jews, and children in Rome.
1544–45	Constitutions begun. Spiritual Diary written.
1550	First draft of Constitutions completed.
1551	Initial approval of Constitutions. Letter of resignation. Founding of Roman College.
1552–54	Ill health. Active administration.
1555	Continued ill health. Reminiscences dictated.
1556	Death on July 31.
1609	Beatified.
1622	Canonized, along with Francis Xavier, by Pope Gregory XV.

Our Itinerary of Camino de Santiago Pilgrimage and Tour of Ignatian Sites

Paris
Bayonne, France
Saint-Jean-Pied-de-Port
Orisson
Roncesvalles
Zubiri
Pamplona
Puente la Reina
Estella
Los Arcos
Viana
Navarette
Nájera
San Millán de la Cogolla
Santa Domingo de la Calzada
Belorado
Villafranca Montes de Oca
Atapuerca
Burgos
Hornillos del Camino
Castrojeriz
Frómista
Carrión de los Condes
Calzadilla de la Cueza
Sahagún
Mansilla de las Mulas
León
Hospital de Órbigo
Astorga
Rabanal del Camino

*Keeping
Company
with
Saint
Ignatius*

178

El Acebo
Ponferrada
Villafranca del Bierzo
Las Herrerías de Valcarce
Triacastela
Samos
Sarria
Portomarín
Palas de Rei
Melide
Arzúa
Amenal
Santiago de Compostela
San Sebastián
Pamplona
Javier
Manresa
Montserrat
Rome

The Beatitudes of the Pilgrim

These inspiring and thought-provoking *Beatitudes*, along with copies of *A Reflection for the Way* and *Our Father*, are given to pilgrim visitors by the Religious of the Sacred Heart of Jesus, caretaker hosts of the thirteenth-century Church of Saint Stephen in Zabaldika, about nine kilometers from Pamplona, along the Way of Saint James. Today the sisters invite Camino pilgrims to stay in their new parish albergue in Zabaldika, and join them for evening communal prayer and relaxed conversation. Learn more at www.facebook.com/ZabaldikaCaminoSantiago and www.rscj.es/contenido/Casas/Zabaldika/2013_04_zabaldika.pdf.

1. Blessed are you, pilgrim, if you discover that the "camino" opens your eyes to what is not seen.

2. Blessed are you, pilgrim, if what concerns you most is not to arrive, as to arrive with others.

3. Blessed are you, pilgrim, when you contemplate the "camino" and discover it is full of names and dawns.

4. Blessed are you, pilgrim, because you have discovered that the authentic "camino" begins when it is completed.

5. Blessed are you, pilgrim, if your knapsack is empty of things and your heart does not know where to hang up so many feelings and emotions.

6. Blessed are you, pilgrim, if you discover that one step back to help another is more valuable than a hundred forward without seeing what is at your side.

7. Blessed are you, pilgrim, when you don't have words to give thanks for everything that surprises you at every twist and turn of the way.

*Keeping
Company
with
Saint
Ignatius*

180

8.   Blessed are you, pilgrim, if you search for the truth and make of the "camino" a life, and of your life a "way," in search of the one who is the Way, the Truth and the Life.

9.   Blessed are you, pilgrim, if, on the way, you meet yourself and gift yourself with time, without rushing, so as not to disregard the image in your heart.

Blessed are you, pilgrim, if you discover that the "camino" holds a lot of silence; and the silence of prayer; and the prayer of meeting with God who is waiting for you.

Notes

1 Joseph A. Tetlow, SJ, "The Fundamentum: Creation in the Principle and Foundation," *Studies in the Spirituality of Jesuits* Vol 21, No. 4 (September 1989): 9–10.

2 James Martin, SJ, *Between Heaven and Mirth* (New York: Harper One, 1989), 70.

3 David L. Fleming SJ, *The Spiritual Exercises of St. Ignatius: A Literal Translation and a Comtemporary Reading*. The Institute of Jesuit Sources (Saint Louis, 1978), 22.

4 William J. Young, SJ, *Letters of St. Ignatius of Loyola* (Chicago: Loyola University Press, 1959), 187.

5 Quoted by James Martin, SJ, *The Jesuit Guide to (Almost) Everything* (New York: HarperCollins, 2010), 8.

6 Young, *Letters*, 245.

7 Ghezzi, Bert, (Chicago: Loyola Press, 2009), xiv. Quote by Saint Ignatius of Loyola.

8 Ruth Burrows, *Guidelines for Mystical Prayer* (Denville, NJ: Dimension Books, 1980).

9 Christopher K. Hsee, Adelle X. Yang, and Liangyan Wang, "Idleness Aversion and the Need for Justifiable Busyness," *Psychological Science* 21, no.7: 926–30. Reprints and permission: sagepub.com/journalsPermissions.nav. July 2010

10 Diane Keaggy, "Walking the Way of St. James," *Catholic Health World* 1 (Sept. 2011): 4.

11 Clive Staples Lewis, *The Four Loves* (New York: Harcourt Brace Jovanovich Publishers, 1960), 61.

12 Young, *Letters*, 379.

13 Robert Fulghum, *All I Really Need to Know I Learned in Kindergarten* (New York: Villard Books, 1988).

14 Young, *Letters*, 180.

*Keeping
Company
with
Saint
Ignatius*

182

15   Pedro de Ribadeneyra, *Vita Ignatii Loyolae, Volume 1,* Cologne, 1502, 538.

16   Young, *Letters,* 4.

17   Ibid., 11.

18   Ibid., 58.

19   William J. Young, SJ, trans., *St. Ignatius' Own Story* (Chicago: Loyola University Press, 1980), 26.

20   Young, *Letters,* 19.

21   *Desiderata* is a prose poem written in 1927 by Max Ehrmann, an American writer and poet from Terre Haute, Indiana. Copyright 1952.

22   Young, *St. Ignatius' Own Story,* 47.

23   Young, *Letters,* 51, 94, 158.

24   Ibid., 269.

25   Marcus J. Borg, *The Heart of Christianity: Rediscovering a Life of Faith* (New York: HarperCollins, 2003), 155–61.

26   Young, *Letters,* 417.

27   Ibid., 319.

28   Ibid., 99.

29   Ibid., 222.

30   Ibid., 412.

31   Ibid., 55.

32   Chip and Dan Heath, *Switch* (New York: Broadway Books, 2010), 50–51.

33   Young, *Letters,* 122.

34   William Melczer, *The Pilgrim Guide to Santiago de Compostela* (New York: Italica Press, 1993), 54.

35   John Brierley, *A Pilgrim's Guide to the Camino de Santiago* 6th ed. (Findhorn, Scotland: Camino Guides, 2010), 274.

36   "A Chance for All to Encounter Christ: Message from Pope Benedict XVI for the Compostela Holy Year 2010," from *L'Osservatore Romano,* Weekly Edition in English (January 13, 2010), 15.

37 Joseph A. Munitiz and Philip Endean, eds. and trans., *Saint Ignatius of Loyola: Personal Writings* (London: Penguin Books, 1996), 292.

38 John C. Olin, *The Autobiography of St. Ignatius Loyola* (New York: Fordham University Press, 1993).

39 See www.santuariodeloyola.org.

40 Linda B. Hall, *Mary, Mother and Warrior: The Virgin in Spain and the Americas* (Austin: University of Texas Press, 2004), 4.

41 Ibid., 4.

42 Ana María Pineda, "Hospitality," in, *Practicing Our Faith*, Dorothy C. Bass (San Francisco: Jossey-Bass Publishers, 1997), 29–42.

43 Joan Segarra Pijuan, SJ, *Manresa and Saint Ignatius of Loyola* 3 ed. (Manresa: Bausili, 1992), 139.

44 Frommer's is a travel guidebook series founded by Arthur Frommer in 1957. See www.frommers.com.

45 Young, *Letters*, 315.

46 Ibid., 240.

47 William A. Barry, SJ, *Paying Attention to God: Discernment in Prayer* (Notre Dame, IN: Ave Maria Press, 1990), 23.

48 Ralph Waldo Emerson, *The Complete Works.* (New York: Houghton, Mifflin, 1904; Bartleby.com, 2013). See www.bartleby.com/90.

49 See caminoignaciano.org.

50 "On the Pilgrimage to Places Linked to Salvation History," a letter of Pope John Paul II published June 29, from *L'Osservatore Romano*, Weekly Edition in English (July 7, 1999): 6–7.

51 Richard Rohr, *Falling Upward: A Spirituality for the Two Halves of Life* (San Francisco: Jossey-Bass, 2011).

52 Dietrich Bonhoeffer, *Letters & Papers from Prison* (New York: Touchstone, 1997), 487.

53 Young, *Letters*, 332.

Index

about paraclete press

Who We Are

Paraclete Press is a publisher of books, recordings, and DVDs on Christian spirituality. Our publishing represents a full expression of Christian belief and practice—from Catholic to Evangelical, from Protestant to Orthodox.

We are the publishing arm of the Community of Jesus, an ecumenical monastic community in the Benedictine tradition. As such, we are uniquely positioned in the marketplace without connection to a large corporation and with informal relationships to many branches and denominations of faith.

What We Are Doing

Books | Paraclete publishes books that show the richness and depth of what it means to be Christian. Although Benedictine spirituality is at the heart of all that we do, we publish books that reflect the Christian experience across many cultures, time periods, and houses of worship. We publish books that nourish the vibrant life of the church and its people—books about spiritual practice, formation, history, ideas, and customs.

We have several different series, including the best-selling Paraclete Essentials and Paraclete Giants series of classic texts in contemporary English; Voices from the Monastery—men and women monastics writing about living a spiritual life today; award-winning poetry; best-selling gift books for children on the occasions of baptism and first communion; and the Active Prayer Series that brings creativity and liveliness to any life of prayer.

Recordings | From Gregorian chant to contemporary American choral works, our music recordings celebrate sacred choral music through the centuries. Paraclete distributes the recordings of the internationally acclaimed choir Gloriæ Dei Cantores, praised for their "rapt and fathomless spiritual intensity" by *American Record Guide*, and the Gloriæ Dei Cantores Schola, which specializes in the study and performance of Gregorian chant. Paraclete is also the exclusive North American distributor of the recordings of the Monastic Choir of St. Peter's Abbey in Solesmes, France, long considered to be a leading authority on Gregorian chant.

Videos | Our videos offer spiritual help, healing, and biblical guidance for life issues: grief and loss, marriage, forgiveness, anger management, facing death, and spiritual formation.

Learn more about us at our website: www.paracletepress.com, or call us toll-free at 1-800-451-5006.

SCAN TO READ MORE

Catching Fire, Becoming Flame
A Guide for Spiritual Transformation
Albert Haase, OFM
ISBN: 978-1-61261-297-3 | $16.99, Paperback

Albert Haase gives the tools and kindling to prepare for the spark of God in your life—and shows how to fan it into flame. This book glows with time-tested wisdom as an experienced spiritual director shares the secrets of the saints. This eminently practical book functions like a personal spiritual retreat.

Catching Fire, Becoming Flame
[DVD]
Albert Haase, OFM
ISBN: 978-1-61261-295-9
Running Time: 180 minutes | $89.95, DVD

There are six thirty-minute segments on this six-session video presentation. A discussion guide and reflection questions are included for small group or personal study or retreat.

1. Spiritual journey as a process of transformation
2. Your image of God
3. The examen
4. The 7 principles of prayer
5. The challenge of forgiveness
6. God's will

ALBERT HAASE, OFM, is a former missionary to mainland China and the award-winning author of six books. He is a preacher in parish missions, presenter of spirituality workshops, spiritual director, and co-host of "Spirit and Life" on the Relevant Radio Network. Visit his website at www.AlbertOFM.org.

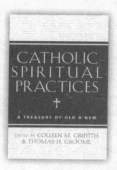

Catholic Spiritual Practices
A Treasury of Old and New
Edited by Colleen M. Griffith &
Thomas H. Groome
ISBN: 978-1-61261-565-3 | $18.99, Hardcover

This collection by today's most respected Catholic writers offers a compendium of practices, traditional and contemporary, that can enable us to sustain and grow a vibrant spiritual life. This must-have volume will quickly become a trusted companion for an entire lifetime of engagement with the beauty and richness of the Catholic faith.

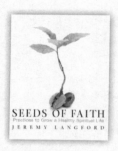

Seeds of Faith
Practices to Grow a Healthy Spiritual Life
Jeremy Langford
ISBN: 978-1-55725-439-9 | $15.95, Paperback

Seeds of Faith by Jeremy Langford covers an astonishing variety of spiritual practices, and does so in such a joy-filled and inviting way that we instantly feel at home.
—Richard J. Foster, author of *Celebration of Discipline* and *Life with God*

Jeremy Langford's multiple talents as a superb writer, a loving father, a dedicated worker, and an ardent believer, combine to make his new book perfect for anyone seeking to lead a faith-filled life in the real world.
—James Martin, SJ, author of *My Life with the Saints*

Available from most booksellers or through Paraclete Press:
www.paracletepress.com • 1-800-451-5006
Try your local bookstore first.